AMERICA - ONE NATION UNDER TYRANTS?

Copyright 2010 by Joe Callihan

ISBN # 978 - 0 - 9821845 - 6 - 1

PUBLISHED BY: FIRE OF LOVE BOOKS LLC

St. Petersburg, Florida 33707

ACKNOWLEDGEMENTS

Although I receive the cover designs for each of my books from the inspiration of the Holy Spirit, I must acknowledge the help I received in bringing the image in my mind's eye to life. Therefore, I am pleased to acknowledge the assistance I received from Ms. Leta Perry, of Columbia City, Indiana, for her digital expertise in making this cover as terrific as it is.

The Cover design for America One nation Under – Tyrants depicts the valuable loss of freedoms and liberty, which will become dead and buried, perhaps forever, should we condescend to allowing godless tyrants take authority in America. The purpose of this book, is to ask of every reader, is it worth the price? Tyrants offers to expose the reasons behind how we have slumped so low, nearing the loss of our country and those things which for hundreds of years, have made us Great among the nations of the world.

Tyrants also offers hope, as ideas and restored ideals bequeathed to us by our founding fathers, come alive once more in the hearts of American Patriots. We can once more be a great nation among the nations of the world. But it will not come easy, nor will it happen overnight. It will require the willingness of every American who loves their country, to depose any and every "would be" tyrant, from ever holding office in America. It will require enlightening the ignorant voters among us. It will require awakening the apathetic, and motivating them into taking positive action. It will require men and women of integrity and honor, to replace lifetime "politicians," and turn America again over to "We the People!" This is the lofty goal of America – One Nation Under Tyrants. Please share this goal with others.

TABLE OF CONTENTS
AMERICA, ONE NATION UNDER TYRANTS?

AMERICA, ONE NATION UNDER TYRANTS?
Copyright 2010 by Joe Callihan
ISBN # 978 - 0 - 9821845 - 6 - 1

PUBLISHED BY: FIRE OF LOVE BOOKS LLC

DEDICATION

This book is dedicated with love and respect to the many people who helped forge my beliefs in good over evil. First, my loving Grandparents, who from my first year, raised me as their son. Then there were boyhood heroes, such as: Superman, Batman, "The Duke" – John Wayne, Roy and Dale Rodgers, who taught me that with courage, good can and will triumph over evil. Also to Clayton Moore – The Lone Ranger, and Jay Silverheels – Tonto, who showed me justice will prevail, and my Indian friends were not ignorant savages; but men and women of integrity, warmth, friendship, and sincerity.

Then there were those who helped influence my teenage years and early adulthood. People like Gerald & Beulah Derstine (my spiritual mentors), Jim Bakker, Dr. Billy Graham, James Robison, and Pat Robertson, The late, Dr. Jerry Falwell, D. James Kennedy; and the many other men and women of God, who proclaim the Gospel under the influence of the Spirit of Truth.

There are of course those whose lives stand out like shinning beacons of hope. The late Dr. Martin Luther King, who proved for the world to see, one possessing Faith in God and courage to take a stand for Righteousness, can make a big difference in the hearts of men, even if it cost him his life. And our late, GREAT President, Ronald Reagan, a man who talked Mr. Gorbochev into "Tearing down that wall of shame." Mr. Reagan was an example of the kind of leadership we so desperately need today, one seeking the guidance of the One True God each day. A Christian (not in label – but in "fruit"), a Patriot, Statesman, Proud American, and family man first – lastly a Politician. He did not go around bowing, or kissing behinds, apologizing for the greatness of America. He sought to see the defeat of Communism, and the promotion of Democratic ideals in the world. Not the reverse, as we are suffering through today.

It is so easy for me to dedicate this book to such heroes. They helped me form the opinions upon which America – One Nation Under Tyrants is based. There are so many others whom I left out, only due to lack of space.

It is my sincere hope that Tyrants will help bring back to life, the desire to see America once again attain its place of greatness in the world. This is not a dream. It can come true. But only as each of us are willing to work at restoring America to the Providence and Guidance of the One TRUE God! If you are one whom this truth hurts and offends, I'm sorry for you. But I will never let go of the One True God, to appease you and all of the false gods of satan and man on earth!

MAY THE ONE TRUE GOD INSPIRE THE HEART OF EVERY READER! NO TYRANT WILL BE TOLERATED IN AMERICA!

INTRODUCTION
ISN'T IT TIME?

America – One Nation Under Tyrants is not an easy book to read. Many of its revelations will raise the ire of controversy, especially among the naive and those wishing to remain blissfully ignorant. The Communist element among us will decry its good old American values of wanting to inspire Honesty, Integrity, and Honor once again, to the American Political scene.

Just like the millionare that paid $250,000.00 for a work of art proved to be a forgery, many of the ignorant will profess the truth to be lies, choosing denial as a way of life. They do so, simply because pride will not allow them to admit they have been taken in by lying politicians.

My response to any and all criticism of Tyrants is: Isn't it time the truth was told? Isn't it time lies and deceptions were exposed for what they are? Isn't it time someone took a stand for restoring foundational American values, such as Honesty, Integrity, and Courage? Isn't it time we kicked Communist Butts out of the American political scene? Isn't it time we worked hard to restore America to greatness once again, among the nations of the world?

The obvious answer to these questions is, not only is it time – it is way past time we, the American people, took back the leadership of our country from Communist hands. My goal is not to offend the naïve or ignorant among us, but to open their eyes to the truth. Those receiving the truth will be set free by it. But those finding the truth to be offensive will find many ways of attempting to use lies, in order to continue living in their imaginary world.

But those willing to stand up for the truth, will happily sing, "God Bless America" and will dare any to silence them. Those who cherish the country our forefathers bequeathed to us will proclaim **boldly**, proudly, and without fear: **IN GOD WE TRUST!** Those having a patriot's heart and love for America will arise and take America back from Communist hands which seek to destroy her.

It is time we brought a swift end to America's decline: spiritually, morally, politically and economically. It is time we choose giving America's posterity; providence and authority back to the One True God under Whose guidance the greatest country upon the earth, was forged in freedom and conceived in liberty. It is time for restoring dignity to the office of the President, for respecting just laws and judges, and for the destruction of unjust laws, and removal of unjust judges. It is time the will of "We the People" not be just heard, but it honored by those we permit to hold positions of authority. It is time for the removal of unjust judges – those giving out mild sentences to heinous offenders, while unjustly sentencing the innocent (like Terri Schivo) to die.

"America – One Nation Under Tyrants?" is a call to every American who truly loves America. No longer must we say, "It is time." We must begin to take the time, make the time and make the effort to reclaim America from the death grip of her domestic enemies. This book is a call to battle, to awaken those in apathy from their dullness, which has allowed tyrants to creep into our government, schools, and justice system. The battle plan is simple: use your power to remove unjust judges and Communist teachers from their position. Use your vote to kick out and replace immoral, power hungry politicians with statesmen and women having a patriot's heart and love for America.

To any who might be offended by the truths you find revealed in Tyrants, I say you have the Constitutional liberty to feel offended by the truth. But spiritually speaking, you have the right to know the truth and to face the truth. For it is in knowing the and accepting truth, you are able to be set free from having conflict with the truth

The goal of this author is to use the truth to expose lies, deceptions, and "spins," which threaten to destroy the foundation and future security of America. Our country was established upon truths which are considered to be self evident. Today, many of those self evident truths have become buried in lies, taught by Communists within our educational system. Today it is considered to be "politically incorrect" to expose lies and promote truth. It is supposedly a fearful thing to be "politically incorrect." Too bad! I do not fear Communist, socialist, or any other form of misguided person choosing to serve satan. I will speak the truth in Love. Love for God, my fellowman, and America – my cherished homeland.

America is not just my country, it is our country. If "We the People" continue closing our eyes in apathetic silence, we will lose our precious freedom of loving and serving the One True God. This was the main foundational belief which helped the early colonists fight to establish the freedom of worshipping the One True God without oppression. If we today are lacking the commitment our forefathers had, then we soon will lose this freedom. If you know, love, and serve only the false gods of satan and man's imagination, you will be saying, "Good!" But if you know, love and serve the One True God, you will say, "There is no way I am willing to sit by and watch this happen!"

WAKE UP! KEEP AMERICA – **ONE NATION UNDER GOD!**

Chapter One
WHAT IS AMERICA'S DESTINY?

The idea for the title of "America - One Nation Under Tyrants?" comes from a quotation attributed to the early American colonist William Penn. "Any people unwilling to be governed by God are destined to be governed by tyrants." Is this the destiny America is presently facing? Looking at the downward course America has been traveling on for over half a century, one would feel the hopeless answer would surely be yes.

I have watched as decade by decade America has moved further away from the Creator Who birthed this country in liberty. When I was a little boy, America was a beacon of light to the rest of the world. The fire of liberty was burning strong in the hearts of a people who knew their liberty was a precious gift from the One **True** God.

In World Wars I and II Americans were called upon to not only defend our own liberty, but to restore it for people in far off lands. American soldiers performed valiantly, marching ever toward victory through their boundless faith in God. Again in the 1950's, Americans were called upon to protect and defend the people of South Korea from tyranny. As part of a multinational force, American soldiers served with a degree of distinction and honor which stood out among the nations of the world.   In the early 1950's, a grateful nation decided to give honor where it was due. Under the leadership of President Eisenhower, Congress passed what would seem a simple, natural, and historically correct statement: Under God was added to our pledge of allegiance. Appropriately, those two words followed the phrase, "one nation." Nowhere in our nation's history did this now **completed** phrase appear foreign to America's foundation. What truths did Thomas Jefferson say were self evident? In America's foundation, were there not to be certain "rights" which are to be cherished and protected? A truly great nation arose from the Godly principles America's foundation was built upon.

For the first 175 years of our existence, it has been common and reasonable for Americans to give honor to the One True God - the "Creator," Who has endowed Americans with unalienable freedoms. Freedoms we have been willing to fight and die to maintain. This could never happen where the people did not love their country, with a patriot's heart.

Today, we are being told it is wrong and evil to desire to give honor to the One **True**

1

God in Whom we supposedly put our trust. We are also being told America is responsible for every short coming of other nations – how stupid is that! What an insult to those brave patriots who risked everything to bring forth a strong nation forged in liberty and freedom. They willingly gave their lives, pledged their homes, allegiance, and money. They were willing to do this because of their unfailing faith that under guidance of the One **True** God, America's foundation would be built. They knew His name was not "buddha," "allah," "Oscar," "Fred," or "whoopee-do". Our founding fathers knew Him as the God of Love, Truth, Life and Light; ingredients without which, no nation can aspire to attain blessings, wisdom, and true greatness.

For the first 175 years America was truly blessed by God. Its noble people honored God with songs of the American spirit. Songs such as Mine Eyes Have Seen the Glory of the Coming of the Lord; My Country Tis of Thee, America the Beautiful, and God Bless America. Songs which inspire love of both the One True God and country, songs which brought honor and patriotism to the heart's of brave and courageous soldiers fighting to keep America free. Aren't you glad we do not have to sing, "My Country is of buddha"? Or, "allah shed his darkness on thee"? In some nations of the world they are singing, "allah curse America!" Of course as long as we know how to sing "God Bless America" with conviction in our heart, allah will never succeed in cursing America.

America's patriotic leaders helped our country grow in greatness among the nations of the world. America was the goal of peoples in almost every other land. To be able to move to America and become a noble American citizen, this was the dream of so many of our ancestors. Our Statue of Liberty was presented by a French people who loved and admired America and what it stood for. Even this great gift has a Christ like saying on it. For it does not say, "give us your rich, your strong, your over fed." What it does say, speaks well for a people wishing to attain greatness, in both the sight of God and man. "Give me your poor, your tired, and your hungry." (I suppose now, the aclu will want to see that "Christian" – "Christ like" remark removed). Well, I've got bad news for them. They'll have to fight me, and millions of other proud American Christians to do it!

We all know that America is the melting pot of the world. America has become a nation where people of all colors, religious beliefs, and nationalities should never fear belief in allah, buddha, Howard, Ralph, or Fred, will be imposed on them by an oppressive government. This has been the cornerstone of America's freedom. It is an essential key to the foundation of a democratic society.

This basic freedom is not the problem. The true problem lies within the heart of the Lazy Christian and Jew in America. We have the freedom by our words and actions of

2

Love, shown to those believing in "buddha," "allha," "charlie," "devil," or "evil;" to introduce them to the <u>Only</u> <u>True</u> <u>God</u> of Love, Light, Abundant Life, Hope, Peace, and Joy. But how very few ever exercise this freedom! How few Christians are taught from the pulpit how to be a powerful witness of Who Jesus is!

Please note, I did not say or imply we had the freedom to force others to know, love, and serve, the One True God. We have only the freedom and responsibility to introduce others to Him, through our actions and words of Love – not self-righteous judgment. This is particularly true of Christians; commissioned by Jesus to be a witness of His kind of Love to the entire world. Demonstrating the Love of God to others is also true of the Jew who understands the meaning of the greeting, "Shalom!" Both Christians and Jews are to be interested in obeying the Ten Commandments (eleven for the Christian), and especially the first two.

I refer you now to chapter two which asks the question, **"What Happened?"**

Chapter Two
WHAT HAPPENED?

Over the past fifty years I have sadly watched as the America I was born into has eroded in moral decay. America has been descending from being a tower of light, into the depth of darkness. There was a brief flicker of light, when for eight years Ronald Reagan, the "great communicator," briefly led America on the path of hope and light. I'll cover that more later.

I have watched the moral decline of the once great nation I love. In the late 1950's "censorship" became the great issue. The losing result was pornographic materials were ruled suitable for only the sophisticated (**sick**) "adult" (**Spiritually ignorant**) mind. Those protesting and not appreciating such "art" because of its immoral content did so merely because they were "unsophisticated children." The porno industry had a "ratings system" supposedly imposed upon it, to placate those opposed to filth being made readily available to their children.

But did this "ratings system" really stop minors from viewing pornographic movies? We all know the answer is (home of satan) no! The so called "ratings system" was just a cleverly designed deception of satan to destroy the minds and souls of young and old alike. Thanks to letters such as "R" (Restricted), "A" (Adults Only), "X" (contains immoral filth), "XX" (contains even more filth), and "XXX" (for very sick minds only); such "Ratings" became a cleaver marketing tool. Now kids could brag about the depth of depravity they had accomplished. "So you went to an "X" rated movie? That's nothing! I went to see a triple "X" movie." These letters became the material of "bragging rights" among the deceived minds of America's youth. Unfortunately, today they still are.

How about the "would be" "adult"? I am appalled when I see an explanation of why some movies are rated unsuitable for minors, yet suitable for would be "adults:" **Contains Nudity, Sex, Violence, and adult? Language!** All of these wonderful adjectives proudly announce only the "adult" mind is prepared to deal with immorality in an "objective" manner. I don't know about you, but to me, being labeled an "adult" means you have gained a degree of "maturity" which a child has yet to attain. Being an **adult** means you have learned how to apply wisdom in deciding issues relating to what is of value in your life. I may be "old fashioned," but to me **sophistication** is being able to discern and throw out **garbage**, accepting only that which is of real value. One who is "unsophisticated" is one who accepts "garbage" and feeds on it, while throwing out

4

the t-bone steak.

This being the case, please answer a few questions if you would? #1) How does the prurient watching the display of a naked human body add value to your life? The truth is it only weakens your control over your flesh. It drives your flesh to indulge in immoral behavior. #2) How does watching couples on the screen fictionally married or not, having sex, make you appreciate this very special gift from God? The truth is it degrades and makes "common" something which God intended to be shared in a beautiful and intimate way between a husband and wife.

Watching sex performed as a casual sport, causes many a husband or wife to view sex as an O.K. past time. If you are married and feel lonely, having a "need" to be "loved" (what a phony use of the word), why let the vows you made before God get in the way of your "satisfaction"?

Sex is a wonderful way for a husband and wife to speak Love to one another when practiced as God intends. Intimacy and faithfulness are so much more than just words. How few understand what intimacy really means. It means I desire to speak Love to my wife (husband) in a very **special** and <u>**exclusive**</u> way. Being faithful means "Honey, there is no other woman (man), who has captured my heart as you have. In thanksgiving to God for bringing you into my life, I will be intimately faithful, in speaking the wordless language of Love <u>only</u> to you, for all the days of my life."

I know what you're thinking, Joe you are too much of a "Romantic." I'll gladly confess I am indeed a "Romantic." (With a capital "R")! I believe in the end, we "Romantics" will get a lot more joy out of our love life. It's like they say about breathing, look at the alternative if you decide to stop. You see you can stop being a "Romantic," but at what cost? Believing "Love" is something very special God intends you to share with your wife (husband), who is someone equally special He intends to bring into your life. Understanding how to <u>Truly</u> <u>Love</u> to the fullest, makes sharing sex the joyful fulfillment God intended.

Such belief is a treasure of great value! We should cherish and nourish such belief into bearing fruit one day, as we find that gift from God – our wife or husband. But try to find <u>True</u> <u>Love</u> in the kinds of movies Hollywood makes today. You can't even find "romance"! satan wants everyone believing "Romance is dead!" In the "love" stories on the screen today, the guy says, "I like your body, I think I love you, come on, let's go to bed!" The women are supposed to go, "He's so <u>sexy</u>, **for such an empty headed bozo**! Just look at his beautiful long hair, it's longer than mine, and how about those "sexy" earrings he wears in his ear, nose, tongue, lip and eye brows?"

Excuse me! I ask, what happened to Love and Romance??? What happens if you decide to stop breathing long enough? You are dead! The same thing happens to those who refuse to allow their emotions to believe in Love and Romance. They become dead to the concepts of intimate fidelity. They become the one using others just for "kicks." I know this is so, because for a long time, I had given up on both Love and Romance. I had been emotionally betrayed, and as many do, I let satan deceive me. I decided I'll never be hurt again, I won't believe in either Love or Romance. In other words, I emotionally held my breath. As the result, I became emotionally dead. I spent many lonely years being a user. I used others, and was used by others who were just as hurt, confused, and emotionally empty as I was.

Sex was not a joyful thing, a brief, momentary physical pleasure, accompanied by the emotional pain of knowing there was no Love present before, during, or after. Sex without Love, Fidelity, and the Commitment of Marriage, is so emotionally empty. Rather than the exciting "sport" (satan had promised), sex became to me, a waste of my valuable time. With lonely tears of desperation, I would cry out in the night to God. "Why can't I just Love and be Loved the way You intended?" But satan turned that plea into another deception, as no woman came along to answer my cry, he said, "See, you've sinned too much for God to Bless your life with someone special to Love!"

But Praise God! One day I realized just how badly I had let God down in allowing satan to guide my flesh. I changed my plea. Instead of concentrating on "my" hurt, I gave attention to God's pain, in having to see His son missing the joy He had planned for his life. I asked Jesus to forgive me, and received His forgiveness! One day, in a very special way, God raised this <u>dead</u> <u>Romantic</u> back to life. To any who understand, may have lived, or are now living in the hellish nightmare of misusing sex; please believe me there is still hope for your life. What Jesus did in my life, He can and will do in yours. You too can be raised from the emotionally empty dead! As you read the last chapter of this book, I will tell you how. If you feel the need to go there now, I won't tell. Besides, don't worry, it's not against the "law"! The rest of these words won't hop off the pages and into your heart until they are read.

Now, can you handle a question about the value of watching on screen violence? Sure such things occur in "real life" everyday, and you can't hide from it. So what? Does that mean you have to welcome it into your life, and/or your home? As a Christian, I am to desire becoming a man who chooses to walk in the Spirit. This means I am to desire to walk in Love, Peace, Forgiveness, Longsuffering (patience), and Joy. However, acts of violence tend to make our flesh desire to give in to anger and revenge.

I can remember having seen each of the late Charles Bronson's "Death Wish" movies. I remember how my flesh responded as he would kill the "punks" who had raped and murdered his wife, and raped his daughter in such a violent way, she had to be institutionalized. As one by one Charlie took them out, my flesh would be cheering him on. I can still remember thinking, "He's being too kind. If I were him, I would give each one of these "punks" a painfully long and lingering agony of death." Can you see where these movies were helping me become Super Christian? I can't! Was I choosing to walk in the "flesh" or in the "Spirit"? That's a no brainer! Watching such violence encourages the flesh to attack our soul and spirit. satan uses such movies to promote our desire to become a slave to following his ways as a means of dealing with life's challenging "realities."

As far as foul mouth demonic language is concerned, if you have read any other of my books, you already know how I feel about this subject. The use of such language is definitely **not** the sign of an "adult." A true adult knows how to communicate in an intelligent manner. Allowing a spiritual moron demon to direct the words flowing from your mouth is **not** a sign of intelligence. Neither is using God's name in vain.

If it angers you to have this fact presented to you, and perhaps you may even desire to curse me out. If this is the case, then you need to get a grip on reality my friend, the same as I had to. I too once used to allow moronic demons to lead my choice of selecting the words coming from my mouth. You need to ask yourself, just as I had to do, who is in control of your tongue? You also need to decide whom you wish to be your Lord and Master - God, your flesh, or dumb little satan? But consider this - your decision has great influence on where you are building your eternal home, and the materials with which you are building it.

Chapter Three
AGAIN I ASK - WHAT HAS HAPPENED

Along came Rowe vs. Wade. The Supreme Court decided rather than <u>interpret</u> the law, they would **make** a law. Thus the evil concept of "abortion" became an American abomination to flaunt before God. The sick, misguided, ego fed minds of the members occupying that "would be" <u>supreme</u> court, declared the law of man's immoral flesh had precedent over the law of a Holy God. God was still allowed to be the "Creator" of life. But if He happened to create a life by "mistake," a life which could "inconvenience" the self centered life of a woman whose responsibility it was to carry and care for that innocent life she had caused to be created; then man in his infinite wisdom, has the "right" to help God correct <u>His</u> **Mistake** through murdering that innocent little life.

The problem here is evident, that little human being is not just a "piece of tissue." Neither is it a "tadpole" which will become a frog or a "caterpillar" that will morph into a butterfly. From conception that life is one of a human being, one to whom God has given a body, soul, and spirit. He has a wonderful plan for that life. God's plan is similar to the one stated by Thomas Jefferson, the unalienable right to life, liberty, and the pursuit of happiness.

Without any doubt, I would say that bunch of <u>would be</u> **Supremes** overstepped their authority. They are not to be looked upon as heroes, but rather a group of zero's. They, in their own little minds, were 250 on the "intellectual" scale. Yet in reality they were zero, in their knowledge of and respect for the God Whom America was founded to be guided by.

In the 60's we had the "undeclared war" called **Viet Nam**. I was almost involved in that mess. While on active duty in the Navy during the late 60's, I was first placed on a ship which was preparing to go to Viet Nam. But my grandmother prayed I would not have to go. Guess what? Orders came in my name, stating I was to be transferred to Panama for shore duty. I later helped arrange that ship's transit of the Panama Canal en route to Viet Nam. Don't tell me prayer has no power!

The ugly truth about Viet Nam has yet to be exposed. Isn't it time someone exposed it? First, in the late 1950's, President Eisenhower in response to the request of a fellow SEATO (South Eastern Asian Treaty Organization) country sent a few "advisors" to the country of South Viet Nam. The mission of these "advisors" was to offer military strategic planning to South Viet Nam's military. The South Vietnamese were engaged in what was then a civil war against the North, which wished to impose Communism upon the people of the South.

I can remember the political flack with which the newspapers attacked the

Eisenhower administration. It happened when a handful of "advisors" were killed in action against the Communist gorillas. In response, the Eisenhower administration reported those killed had been guilty of disobeying orders. We were told they supposedly had been given strict orders forbidding their active participation in combat conditions. Their orders were to "advise" only, staying far behind the lines of battle.

From my own military experience I have learned we can't believe everything the government tells us. However the truth of what happened during the Kennedy administration sticks out like a sore thumb. Under Kennedy the true, now perverted purpose of Viet Nam was revealed. Shortly after taking office, with Kennedy, **escalation** became the operative word concerning Viet Nam. Although the truth remains well guarded and hidden, it is my sincere belief that one day the secretary of defense Mac Namara, along with the Head of the Joint Chiefs of Staff approached Kennedy with some alarming news. Many of the men who had served in WWII and Korea were aging. As the result, many were retiring after twenty years of service. The new crop of officers and enlisted had no actual combat experience. The only method of training they had received was **war games**, with the emphases on the word **games**. We were in the dangerous military position of having a depleting "battle hardened" force. "Battle Hardened" referring to those having experienced actual combat, and thus more comfortable in battle than the raw recruit would be.

In addition, we had developed a large array of new high tech weapons. The only problem being, we did not know how well they might work in actual combat conditions. The fear was we might be wasting taxpayer dollars on systems which might not function properly under actual combat situations. Such weapons needed proving to determine if they were useful or useless in combat. I believe they then pointed out to President Kennedy what a great opportunity Viet Nam offered in resolving these issues.

America proceeded to use Viet Nam and its people as a means of testing new battlefield strategies and technologies, while building up a supply of young battle hardened troops. Viet Nam became a way of building America's military might. This is why only the forces needed to **maintain** status quo were sent into Viet Nam. Never was the kind of force deployed which could assure victory, allowed to become involved in this "conflict," this "undeclared war." The obvious use of a two year rotation of troops proves "war games" were being conducted for real. (In the 1980's Russia chose using Afghanistan in much the same way we had Viet Nam, for similar goals and reasons).

In offering this discourse I have come across Kennedy worshipers. They have declared to me, "Kennedy would never do such a thing! He had experienced war himself, and knew first hand of its horrors." I always ask them to look at who his idol

9

was. President George W. Bush when first campaigning stated very boldly Jesus Christ was whom he looked to as an role model. In the 1960's Kennedy announced that James Bond - 007 was his idol. Which among these two would indicate a clandestine mind, capable of using Viet Nam to play **war games** for real?   Because of the stain of the Mei Lai massacre and other horrific events, Viet Nam is often referred to as the "unjust" and "immoral" war. The consequence of this image and use of such labels have placed the stigma of disgrace upon the soldiers who were called upon to participate in Viet Nam. I ask: **Have any critics ever considered the immense bravery of those who served in Viet Nam?** It took far more bravery than running scared to Canada! How about looking to Kennedy and Johnson and asking the question: why did **you** pursue such an **immoral war**?

Today there are still many former soldiers who served in Viet Nam with distinction. Many are still left with the hellish nightmares of a war unlike any we ever had participated in before. There are those who are blind, lost legs, arms, or both, while performing what they believed was their duty to their country. Is it not time to give them the appropriate honor their courageous service to our country has earned? Yes, you may question the motives of their commander in chief. But **never** are you to question the loyalty of America's brave soldiers - to both their commander in chief and their country!

It amazes me that we still have and had in our Congress, people like John Kerry, the band-aid Purple Heart hero, and the late Mr. "foot in his mouth" – John Murtha, both former soldiers who chose to turn into cowards and traitors. Only a sick element in America would keep electing such wimps to "represent" America. To any and ALL who still would throw insults and cast dispersions on those who served in Viet Nam, I say, they paid the price you were too afraid to pay. **So shut your cowardly mouth!** (Sorry - sometimes my flesh desires to minister to the cowardly who would criticize the brave soldiers who did their duty).

Is it not time to say thank you to President Nixon? For all of his human fears and failings, President Nixon looked at Viet Nam in a different light. He could hear the cries of young widows and orphaned children. He could see the pain endured by those who had been maimed. He observed the unrest and division within the heart of America's people over Viet Nam. As President he knew the ugly truth behind Viet Nam.

I can remember the political flack President Nixon endured when he ordered the mining of the harbor leading into Hanoi. The liberal wimps screamed in fear, "There are British and French ships traveling to Hanoi, they are our allies, what if one of them hits a mine?" They cried loudly, as all cowards do. President Nixon's reply was that of a leader having backbone. "If they **are** our "allies," why are they furnishing weapons to our enemy?" He said, "If one of their ships should hit a mine, it's their bad luck for being there." He knew the profit hungry "allies" had no shame or honor when it came to making a buck. I was so proud of his courage. I was even prouder when one day he declared, **ENOUGH!** President Nixon went on to make the effort to get our prisoners of war set free, and extract America in as honorable a way as was available to him. For such courage and compassion we owe him a debt of gratitude. To the people of South Viet Nam, we owe a sincere apology.

The 60's and 70's were turbulent times for other reasons than just Viet Nam. The youth of America were being sold on the saying "sex, drugs, and rock and roll." Out of this hedonistic philosophy came the "sexual revolution." Who cares about God's commandments? If it "feels" good, do it! Filth became common place in America, as in rejecting God and His Holiness, both the movies and hippies became a stench pot of filth. Let's not forget the new and exciting "topless bars." The only proper place for God in the America of the late 60's and 70's was in church buildings. But why visit them? Topless bars were far more **entertaining**!

I can still remember an encounter I had with a "topless bar" in San Diego (you guessed it, the Navy had sent me there). I kept asking the very amply endowed young "lady" (who was dancing on the bar in front of me) for change. First, I gave her a twenty to pay for the Michelob beer I had to order (coke was not on the menu, at least not in the form I was used to). Then it was, "Would you please change a ten," then five ones, then four quarters, until I finally got down to two dimes and a nickel. I would have gone for five pennies, but I kind of sensed from what she said when she brought me the dimes and nickel, the "lady" was getting a little tired of having to bend down in front of me to get and give the change to me. Discerning she must have caught on to my game, I decided not to press my luck any further, so I left. Besides, these guys didn't serve coca cola at any price! From the way they reacted to my asking for a coke, I just knew I'd better not ask for a glass of water. Yes, I know, I was a rascal!

I suppose before I totally destroy my reputation, I'd better make something clear. I'm not advertising "topless bars." In fact, there is only one other time I ever visited such a place. You see first I went out of curiosity (I also was not yet born again). The last time was due to being too trusting. The department store where I was working had their annual awards banquet at a large restaurant in Tampa. My boss offered to drive a carload of his salesmen to Tampa with him. I was assured after the awards banquet had ended, we would go back to the store in St. Pete., where we could drive our car home.

Much to my dismay when the awards presentations had ended, the guys decided to "celebrate" having won a few of the awards. They chose going to a nearby strip joint and topless bar to partake of the "entertainment." By now I had become a born again

11

Christian and felt very uneasy about the whole situation. But like a coward, unfortunately I kept my mouth shut and went along. Once inside, I could not see the sense of putting my hard earned fives, tens and twenties into a girl's underwear, just so I could look at the other guys and give a sheepishly naughty grin. I did order my "coke," but that proved to be a problem. One of our guys having had too much to drink was protesting my having just a coke. Amusing himself, he questioned if I were a man. I chose to ignore his ignorant comments (comments which in my past would have gotten him a bloody nose). But unfortunately he went way past my limit when he threatened to pour some of his drink into my coke.

I politely told him, "You don't want to do anything like that; it would ruin your fun." "Why would it ruin my fun?" he asked. "Because if I were to catch you trying to pour something into my coke, I would take you outside and give you a broken nose, black eye, and maybe knock a tooth or two out." He boldly asked, "Is that a THREAT?" I simply answered, "No, it's just a cold hard fact of life! If I were to catch you trying to pollute my coke, I would have absolutely no remorse in doing a lot of painful physical harm to your body." At this I finished my coke and said, "I think I'll step outside, it's getting a little too stuffy in here for me."

Shortly afterward my boss came outside to where I was standing in the parking lot. "You were a little hard on Ralph, weren't you?" he asked. I replied, "No, actually I went easy on him; I just told him the facts of life. Ed I'm a Christian, and I don't belong in a place like this. I feel very convicted and uncomfortable being in this atmosphere. (In fact, the Holy Spirit had been screaming at me to leave - the minute we had pulled on to the parking lot). So I'm going to call a taxi and go home." He said, "O.K., I understand. I'll tell the guys you got sick and went home." "Tell them whatever you want! I'm out of here!" I then proceeded to walk away.

I had walked down the road a few blocks when a delightful sign offered me refuge. It was an all night bowling alley. I went inside and placed a call to my sister in St. Petersburg. Explaining my predicament in a limited way (avoiding mention of the "topless club" I just had come from), I told her I was stranded, and I asked if she would mind driving to the bowling alley in Tampa to give me a ride back to the store, where I could pick up my car. God Bless her, she said she would be right over. I proceeded to bowl five or six games while I awaited her arrival. I even had another coke (which I enjoyed in peace, and paid a lot less for). Believe it or not, I got much more enjoyment smashing those pins with the bowling ball, than I would have gotten putting my money down a bra or panty, regardless of how well it was filled!

Of course the next day at work I got teased about not being able to hold my coke. Many of the guys were anxious to tease me, except for one, Ralph, the guy I had offered to hurt. When he came to see me I was pleasantly surprised by his comment. "I understand I got a little out of line last night. I want to apologize for it. I guess I had too much to drink. I want to thank you for walking away. I'm sure if it came to it, you would have beaten the hell out of me!" His sincerity and his words moved me so much. "Ralph, that's something I would never want to do, you're a true friend and a great guy."

We have come a long way since then, this country and me. I became "born again," while a sick liberal movement has taken root in American society. It's made up of dumb Leftist creeps, who wish the America I once knew, had never been born at all. I know it's not "nice" to call them dumb creeps, when they're really only dumb Commies. But believe me, compared to what in my flesh I **really** would like to call them - "dumb creeps" is **"<u>NICE</u>"!** I guess the proper "spiritual" term would be, "satanically challenged" people, who allow **dumb demons** to guide their way of thinking.

I know that as a minister of the gospel, my goal should be not to offend. It's just that I'm tired of being **offended** by clowns who think they are going to run my country into Hell. When I was brought up, I was taught **NEVER** to **FEAR** a bully, instead - give them reason to **FEAR** me! I feel the same way toward those offending me by wanting to take away my precious liberties which so many have fought and died to preserve. I want them to understand my message LOUD and CLEAR! You'd better learn how to **FEAR GOD**, and <u>worry</u> about His Loud Mouth servants like me, who will not be silenced by fear of you!

I believe far too many Christian ministers and lay people have been scared into silence for way too long. Far too many have bought into the simple minded deception of, "Duh, it's a <u>free</u> country, freedom of speech you know, what can I do?" I'll tell you what you **can do!** You can get some guts and common sense inside you. **Stand up - make your voice heard!** America's founding fathers never intended for satan and his phony little gods to run rough shod over the wonderful "freedoms" they fought and died to give us. Our precious foundation freedom to give worship, honor and glory to the <u>One</u> <u>True</u> <u>God</u> is worth fighting to preserve. It's time to inform these "misinformed" and "ignorant" people, that **satan has NO freedom in America!** he and **all** of his dumb little gods, have no **"rights"** to chase Christian's and Jews off the scene!

Today, any effort to show the God America was founded upon really does exist, is being called "UN-AMERICAN" by **ignorant** "liberal" judges and Congressmen and women. Christians have sat quietly by as the Ten Commandments were removed from sight, in fear that they might offend someone's conscience. We have watched silently as our children are allowed to have pornographic material in school libraries and condoms

13

readily handed out; while prayer to the One True God is considered dangerous. Why? It is offensive to those believing in satan's false gods, and those of man's imagination. They are forced to learn about Moslem customs, beliefs, and "holy" (?) days; but how dare you mention anything of truth regarding the One True God!

Where will this end? When will it end? How much lower are we to allow this once great country to descend into the depravity of moral decay? How much longer are we as Christians to sit around in **Apathetic Silence**? Who has the guts to speak up? Surely I'm not the only one with the Love of a patriot's heart for America? I'm willing to fight unjust laws imposed by ignorant "would be" judges! I'm willing to challenge them to their face, **prove to me America was not founded to be guided by the One True God!** They can't do it friends, and no amount of lies will change that historic fact. I'm willing to demand that stupid and unqualified judges and politicians resign! We desperately need the "No Confidence" Vote! Are you willing to join me in this fight? Will we win back the America we used to know, the prosperous country of a people who are truly blessed and protected by the hand of the One True God, in Whom we place our Trust?

If you are lacking the guts to take a stand, you may very well risk having to ask "buddha," or "allah," or any of the other false gods of satan, to bless America. Those lacking knowledge of the One True God are more than willing to join the "Wrong" Rev. "Wright"- in asking God to Damn, not Bless America. How Patriotic? No. How STUPID! The more unpatriotic activities and lies which go unchallenged by people who Love America, the closer we are to the day Americans will have decided to flush America down the toilet. Sadly, from the looks of things today we are very close!

To me, that's **UN-AMERICAN!** I opened this book with a quotation made by William Penn. "Any people unwilling to be governed by God, are destined to be governed by Tyrants!" Do you doubt allah is a tyrant? Just ask those whose life will be taken for daring to declare they do not believe in him!

Get this - all you liberal judges and politicians! As an American, I declare my right to worship **only the One True God**, and my freedom to **denounce** the false gods of satan and man's imagination. As an American, I have the freedom to exercise my responsibility to God. I **can** do my best to **Love** my brothers and my sisters (who may be worshiping a false god of satan or man, or no God at all), into the Kingdom of the **One True God**. As an American, I put all who would try to deny me this precious freedom on notice. America's Christians no longer will stand silently by in apathy and permit your denying us the freedom and opportunity of bringing souls out of darkness, and the bondage of fear, lies and deceptions. As an **American** I boldly **SHOUT** with Faith, Hope and Joy,   **MAY GOD BLESS AMERICA!**

14

Chapter Four
AMERICA - ONE NATION UNDER FRED,
BILLY BOB, ED, OR THE UNKNOWN GOD

Further moral erosion has been observed as "religious" symbols are being removed by ignorant judges. This is being done on a scale which would make our forefathers ask of us; "Why are you unwilling to fight for the preservation of the foundation we built America on?"

Today I find the name of the One True God, the Cross of the Savior of the world, and the Ten Commandments, are being removed from sight. We are told they fall into the "illegal" category of being "religious symbols." The problem I have with such reasoning is: **It is nothing more than a big lie!** I make no apology to anyone for saying this!

First, God is not a "religious symbol." He is the Almighty Creator of everything we can see, and that which we cannot see. No "religious symbol" can set the sun, moon, stars, planets, and billions of universes into place and give them order! God made you and me to be His sons and daughters, to enjoy sharing a loving <u>relationship</u> – not <u>religion</u> with Him. You who in ignorance refuse to accept this wonderful **truth** have no authority to replace it with your favorite "lie"!

Secondly, man goofed and fell into sin through disobedience, willfully doing the only thing God had told him not to do. In doing so, he lost the purity of his standing in the sight of a Holy Father. Because of sin, God could no longer look upon us as His son or daughter. But the truth is He Loved us so much, and missed the relationship He had created us to share with Him, He sent His only begotten Son to offer a pure sacrifice on the cross. Jesus took on the punishment we were due to receive. He made the sacrifice of Love on the cross, which by the shedding of His Holy Blood, restored our relationship again, to one of purity in God's sight. All He requires of us is acknowledge we are sinners and need our Savior. Is that asking too much?

The cross of Jesus therefore is **not** a "religious" symbol. The cross is a symbol of a Loving Father and an obedient Son. It is the symbol of the victory of eternal life, over eternal death for you and me. The cross is the symbol of Love and Hope for all mankind! No "religious" symbol could ever offer such strong realities! As we journey in this mortal life on earth, our immortal spiritual life is headed toward eternity. Without accepting the fact that we all have sinned and fallen short of the glory of God, and without accepting Jesus' sacrifice of Love, our eternal destiny is Hell. The cross, upon which Jesus shed His Blood for forgiveness of our sins, is a symbol of Power which no "religion" on earth can offer to man!

Lastly, the Ten Commandments are **not** a "religious" symbol. They offer wisdom as to how we may show our Heavenly Father we truly love Him. Jesus said, **"If you love Me - keep My commandments.** They also offer a way of attaining an abundant life here on earth, as well as storing up eternal treasure in Heaven. The Ten Commandments are not just words written on blocks of stone. All who have accepted the Blood of the new and everlasting covenant, which was fulfilled by Jesus, have found the Ten Commandments are now written on their heart. This is true of every born of the Spirit of God **believer**. If this is not you, it can and should be! I pray that God will use me, or other Christians, to help you seek to become "born again."

satan may have deceived you into not believing the Power and Truth contained in the Ten Commandments. However, no matter hard you may try to deny their Power, and their proper place in America's cherished institutions, your lie is still only a lie!. Without the guidance of God's Commandments as its foundation, justice is just an empty concept.

In these four chapters, moral erosion of the freedoms our founding fathers deeded to our care has been presented as a very clear danger. The effects of moral corrosion, if left unchecked, will have devastating results in how America will be governed in the future. Even today, the morally corrupt government we are currently experiencing offers strong proof of what I am saying. What we choose to do, or fail to do today, will greatly affect the future of our beloved country. In what may seem like a simple yet direct observation, I would offer my assessment as to why all of this kind of "religious" fervor has attempted to destroy faith in the One True God in Whom America was founded.

Because of our great zeal and desire to be known for "religious freedom," "religion" has been permitted to spread its powerless false beliefs in the heart's of many Americans. Today in America cults are a common place reality. Operating under the label of "religious freedom," satan has deceived many regarding their relationship with the One True God. Many are kept from reaching their eternal home in Heaven; choosing by deception to dwell eternally in the home prepared for satan and his demons. We, knowing the truth about our relationship with God, have failed in loving our brothers and sisters enough, to bring them the opportunity of being set free from the bondage of lies, deceptions, and every "religious symbol."

As I stated earlier, we do this not by fear, force, harassment, put downs, or any other unloving words or actions. We are to win souls by the love we show daily to each other and to others. All who have received the Baptism of the Holy Spirit and Fire have within the ability to Love as Jesus Loves. America and the world needs to see the Love of Jesus is **real**, and has far greater **power** than any false god of satan or man's imagination.

The problems we are facing today are mainly due to our long season of apathy. For decades Christians have sat by and watched the moral decline of America. satan has been allowed to roam freely in deceiving the hearts of America's people. Today we are reaping the bounty of our apathetic actions. The cost is high, as we see immoral men and women gaining positions of authority. Those whose god is "Fred," "Billy Bob," "Ed," "self" or "satan," have taken positions of authority which permit trying to force satan's deceptions upon America's Christians and Jews. I make no apology for encouraging Christians and Jews everywhere to take them on, and remove them from power. I do apologize to God and to you for my season of apathy, in allowing such "satanically challenged" people to get control in our country. Enjoy it while you can! You're on your way out! I have awoken from my apathy, and you are in trouble!

Is that a threat? It may sound like one. But actually it is a promise I made to God and to our forefathers, to be vigilant in asking God for the wisdom needed to mount a campaign to remove the "satanically challenged" from office, or to effect a real change in whom they choose to call master and serve. I am tired of having to cast my vote for wolves in sheep's clothing.

In our Congress we have men and women who call themselves "Christian." They will go to a church sometimes for "photo op" days. They even will attempt to lip sync the song, "God Bless America" on the steps of the Capital. They then will prove their desire to follow Jesus by voting against stopping abortion, and proudly speaking out passionately on behalf of homosexual marriage. Christian? I think not! Their fruit stinks too much! Some are simply just outright liars, or as they view themselves, "the consummate politician."

Some are just confused; they wish to serve the "unknown God." The reason these have difficulty pleasing Him is because they do not know Him. Our job is the same one Paul had among the Greeks. We must introduce them to the "unknown God, the One True God of Love, Light, Mercy, Forgiveness, Justice, Truth, and Might. Once they come to know Him they will reverence Him, and desire to follow only His ways. However, there are others who desire to please satan, as they have chosen to serve that dummy as lord. Their place to serve him (if they don't repent), is in Hell - **not in America's seats of power!**

So you can see there is still hope for America to turn back into being "one nation **under God**" again. But it must be a hope which resides within your free will and mine. Are we to awaken from our apathy, and with love introduce others to the One True

God America was founded upon? Are we willing to ask the Holy Spirit to help us lead others from the bondage of "religion," that they may know the powerful relationship the Blood of Jesus restores? I hope and pray we will! The challenge is before us. The future destiny of America is to be found in our response. Will tomorrow find us being governed by tyrants and false gods of satan's design?   What will your answer be? What will you do? What can you do to restore America to once again being truly a nation under the One True God, in Whom we place our trust? If you, like President Reagan, have within more patriotic statesmanship than politician, you might consider running for elected office, or appointment to our court system. But if you are not so inclined, you might consider campaigning for, financially supporting and voting for **only** those who truly are more a God reverencing patriot, than politician.

Remember, due to our apathy in the past satan has had little or no constraint in getting his "goof up's" elected and appointed to positions of authority. As I am writing this chapter it has been reported that a cross erected over seventy years ago in one of our national parks, was ordered to be removed by some little "goof" daring to presume to call himself a "judge." The cross in question had been paid for by a group of WWI veterans. They had seen the godless form of "leadership" found in many foreign countries (like the France of today). They placed the cross to pay respect to the Son of God, Who keeps America free from the godless "leadership" of "religion." (Just look at Iran to see what I'm talking about).

Yes "little would be judge," by all means **remove that cross!** For it surely is a threat to the demonic forces trying to rule in the hearts of America's people! My only question for you "judge" is do you know the Jesus Who suffered and died on that cross for you and for me? If not, can we talk?

O.K., it's time now to read chapter five - if you dare.

Chapter Five
allah IS WAITING IN THE SHADOWS

We can't proclaim religious freedom and leave out allah. Of course we know from observance of countries where allah presides, freedom of any kind is a "foreign" "demonic" concept. No other "religion" is permitted. The Bible, God's Love letter to His children is feared. Where allah is allowed to reign, loving your enemies must never replace hating them. Fear, (not a reverencing kind of fear) a dark and deadly kind of fear, must control the heart of his followers. allah does not seek his followers to obey him because they love him, but rather because they live in the bondage of fearing him. How tragically sad that allah's followers cannot say, "we have not been given a spirit of fear; but of power, love, and a sound mind." (2nd. Timothy, chapter 1, verse 7)

Please tell me, where does allah say, "**Bless** those who curse you, **do only good** to those who hate you, and **pray** for those who despitefully use and persecute you that you may **be** the children of your Father in Heaven?" No, allah says: cowardly murder all who refuse to bow down to me. How clearly we can see Love is of Light and Life; while Hatred is of Darkness and Death. Yet this and every truth about the One True God, are always feared by those embracing the lies and deceptions of satan. Coming to the knowledge of the Truth concerning God through receiving Jesus, His Son, sets the heart free to know Light, Love, Peace, and Joy. Giving worship to allah and his ways of darkness only permit his followers to know hatred, sorrow, despair, death, and war.

Because of the worship of "religious freedom" here in America, today good old allah has madrases's in daily operation. They are schools of hatred, where children are being taught "Christians" are the enemy - they must be stopped at any price! Even if that price is strapping dynamite to your body and killing yourself as well as other innocent men, women, and children. allah's followers are teaching their children to follow after the ways of darkness, fear, hatred, and death. Children are being told, "Christians" are never innocent - even if they are only five seconds old. They are your enemy! To encourage cowardly behavior, a great reward is promised. When you kill a "Christian" sacrificing your own life, satan will reward you with a trip to Heaven (which we know is really spelled H-e-l-l).

All choosing to walk in the Light of God's Love, recognize what blatant lies these are. But to those knowing only the bondage of darkness, hatred, and fear, such lies are readily accepted as truth. Can you not see the need to love such children and their parents away from the bondage of darkness? What can we do about it? We can daily seek the Fruit of the Holy Spirit to be made manifest in our life. Our words and actions of Love have the power to shine Light upon the darkness, if we will only make the effort to seek out and submit to the Fire of Jesus' kind of Love. As we seek for the Kingdom of the One True God to rule and reign in our daily life, we will make a difference. We will be able to overcome the deepest of hatred, offer faith and hope to those ensnared by depression and fear. Therefore, using the Spirit of Truth, we can destroy the bondage of darkness allah has placed in the heart of those in service to him.

Of course attaining the power to do all of this requires commitment, work, and responsibility on our part. Some may be so committed to powerless "religion" they lack understanding of all the gifts of spiritual power which God has available. "Religion" will cause a lack of commitment or desire to risk reaching out in Love to those enslaved by darkness. Many label wearing Christian are comfortable with the kind of apathy which tells them, warming the seat of a pew for one hour "most" Sundays fulfills their only **duty** to God. How about the eleventh commandment give us by Jesus? "Love others, **the same as** I love you." (That's with unconditional and committed L-O-V-E).

To all who use the "pew warming duty" excuse I would caution, allah is waiting in the dark shadows. All he needs to take control, is enough apathetic label wearing Christians to welcome him to lead and guide America. Could such a thing happen? Of course it could! (Take a close look at Obama – Moslem day of prayer, but Christian day is canceled). But I don't want to be a part of helping to make it work for him. I'm willing to fight as a soldier in God's Army to keep America "One Nation Under the **One True God**," not allah, or any other false god!

Soldiers in the True Army of God fight not as the cowardly. The weapons we use not being carnal - are spiritual, and therefore are more powerful than any atomic bomb. Our weapons are formed of the Light, Love, and Word of the One True God! Instead of dealing death, darkness, despair, fear, and destruction, we offer Love, Light, and Life. In believing in the One True God and having His Holy Spirit guide our life, we have the hope of a brighter tomorrow, and restoration of body, soul, and spirit. Having the Holy Spirit inside, we know our body is His Temple, where Truth, Light, Love, and Life reside. Never would we permit satan to turn our body into the source for unholy and cowardly lies, darkness, hatred, and death.

If you who are reading this are currently sold into the bondage of spiritual darkness, hatred, and death, there is hope for you. Your body does not have to remain a temple of doom. All you need to do is just reach out to Jesus. Ask Him to reveal Himself to you. Seek His forgiveness for your sins, just as I and every "born again" believer had to do, and still have to do daily. Ask Jesus to fill your body, soul, and spirit, with the Power of His Holy Spirit, and the Fire of His Love. Jesus Loves you so much more than allah, He will **never** fail you.

Please, give the Holy Spirit the opportunity to bring to your spirit Light, Love and adoption into the family of the TRUE God. If you will do this, He will teach you Who Jesus is, how to seek and find His forgiveness, and how to become endowed with real Power - the Power of Love. The Holy Spirit does not bring you a reason to be in bondage to fear. He gives you the freedom of knowing your "Relationship" with your Father in Heaven is restored. He encourages you to **boldly** approach God in His throne room, calling Him "Abba" (which means Daddy).

You can be set free from the bondage and fear allah has you living under. But you must make a decision to know the Truth, the Way, and the Life - **JESUS**. You must by Faith, ask Jesus into your heart to be your Lord and Savior. God is a rewarder of those who **Diligently** seek Him. May God Richly Bless You! Your brother in Christ, Joe

21

Chapter Six
COME BACK TO THE DOLLAR STORE
RONALD REAGAN

A few years ago a movie was made entitled, "Come Back to the Five and Dime James Dean." I am told it was about die hard fans who lamented the passing away of actor, James Dean. Times have changed the five and dimes are now the dollar stores. America has lost a man of far greater magnitude than James Dean ever was.   It was on Thursday, the week in which America was mourning the passing of one of its greatest leaders, that I first began writing this book. It was 1:00 P.M. as I began writing this chapter in honor of him. As I put these words into my computer file, America's 40th President, Ronald Reagan's casket is on display in our nation's capitol. Many thousands have been passing by to say farewell.

Ronald Wilson Reagan was truly a man of the people. He served the people and the country which overwhelmingly elected him, with a patriot's zeal, and a statesman's fervor, something rarely seen in a "politician." The warmth of his love for America and her people, the hope he had for America's future, and his quick Irish wit, made him very dear to our heart. His accomplishments as President made him a legend among world leaders of the twentieth century. In comment after comment, tribute after tribute, President Reagan was and is referred to as "the great communicator."

This title was earned by a man who knew and truly loved God. He was a Christian man whom the people of America wisely chose to represent their needs, values, and aspirations. As a leader, his job was to inspire values which are pure, encourage goals which help needs to be met, and offer aspirations which lead to hope, rather than despair. To say he did his job well would be an understatement of the facts. Ronald Reagan was an example of what a leader can be. He was first a devout Christian (a follower of Christ – not a "Religious Label Worshiper"), second, a loving husband and father, thirdly, a patriotic and proud American, and lastly a "politician." In other words, he had his priorities in order. Sadly, for most "politicians" that order is reversed. Today, too many shun the very idea of being referred to as a "Christian." Why could that be? Do you suppose it could have anything to do with having to explain their support for homosexual marriage, denouncing the right of children to pray in school, and condoning the wholesale murder of innocent babies for convenience? No "politician" would consider opposing such "issues" as a wise move. Only a Christian Patriot, who truly loves America and the God under Whose Providence she thrives, would dare take such a bold stand against the forces of darkness.

Ronald Reagan was such a man, and America was blessed under his leadership. He earned the title "the great communicator" not from his wisdom in choosing the words of the speeches he made, as most people believe was the criteria. No, he became the "great communicator" because he had the wisdom to seek first God's wisdom in carrying out the awesome duties of the Presidency of the United States. In his desire to guide this nation under God, President Reagan had the ability and desire to listen to the voice of the only true "Great Communicator" - the Holy Spirit. He listened with love, respect, and reverence for His wisdom. He then appropriated the words he had received into the speeches he gave. He also never forgot to inject a bit of Irish humor, but that was his God given heritage of being born Irish.

Was President Reagan the "perfect" Christian leader? No, he made his share of mistakes, as we all do. One of the worst in my mind was when he rightfully pointed out how the Supreme Court in Rowe vs. Wade overstepped their authority, and the boundary they are to operate under. He stated how the Supreme Court had "**made**" a law of "abortion rights" (which is the responsibility of the legislative branch of government). They had blatantly done this rather than "interpret" the law, which is within their authority. There was no law in existence stating you have the right to murder any fellow infant human being, regardless of their residing in their mother's womb. But he lacked the will to seek approval of the American people in correcting this enormous act of tyranny by the Supreme Court.

I can't remember <u>ever</u> asking my representatives to enact a law saying it's a good and moral thing to murder innocent babies by the millions in America, just to placate the self centered desires of irresponsible people. I'm even more certain I never encouraged any court to believe it had the tyrannical power to inflict such an immoral law upon the citizens of the country I love. Today we are paying a very heavy price for that injustice. We are allowing Mexico to flood illegal immigrants into our country. We do so in the hope that somehow they will get jobs, and pay income tax; this being the only way of trying to keep social security viable, as "baby boomers" such as myself, begin to retire in record numbers. The young American work force which would have naturally been around to help meet this need was unfortunately murdered off by the callous, immoral, and cold hearted, who chose walking in darkness.

I say this not in condemnation, but as a matter of fact, not fiction. Praise God, many of those mothers who unwisely chose death, have come to the saving knowledge of Jesus Christ, and have obtained His forgiveness, and His new life. As proof observe the lady whose case prompted Rowe vs. Wade. She now is a devout Christian woman who is stoutly fighting against this horrific act of barbarism.

So we know President Reagan was not perfect. Correct in his statement of fact, yet lacking the courage to get the American people to stand behind demanding this injustice be put to an immediate end. Has America traveled so long on the path of darkness and death they have come to accept this evil disease as a way of life? I hope and pray not! But we've yet to know for sure. I for one, would like to know if Americans still have the courage to demand an immediate ceasing of this practice of satanic worship - offering up the life of innocent babies on the alter of convenience. If they don't, then I would like to see the words, "In God We Trust" removed from our money. If the true meaning of that ideal is no longer written on the majority of American hearts, America's destiny truly lies in the hands of tyrants!

It's been said many times in tribute to President Reagan: "He helped us look to the hope of what America could be, rather than dwell in the despair of our present fears." This is the kind of leadership only a man or woman who is walking close in their relationship with God could inspire in the hearts of America's people. The Ayatollahs of Iran, Saddam Hussain, or Ben Laden could never evoke such high ideals of leadership. Why? Because their god is the prince of darkness, the god of hatred, despair, barbaric evil, and death.

How blessed we are in America to have boldly written on our money, In the God of Light, Love, Hope, and Life, we place our trust. Our money is used in a charitable way, both at home and all over the world. How sad that such money is also used to buy drugs and alcohol, buy and sell pornographic materials, and to pay hit men and women to murder babies for convenience.

If America's economy is ever to become strong, vibrant, and secure again, we must work to reach the hearts of those spending their money on such immoral pursuits. We do so, not by self righteous condemnation, but rather by letting our light so shine before men, that they may see our good works, and glorify our Father which is in Heaven. (Matthew, chapter5, verse 16). If we ever are to achieve President Reagan's vision of being "a light on the hill top," the God America was founded upon must be restored to His proper place in the heart of America's people.   We must have the courage our founding fathers imparted to us as our heritage so long ago. We must **demand** from those chosen to represent what is right for America that the ways of the One True God will continue to be the **only foundation** America builds its hopes upon. From its top leaders, its law makers, its court judges, to the grass root movements, God's ways must become the **only** material we choose to build with!

Tomorrow President Reagan's body will begin its final journey to be buried in California. I hope one day God will allow me to visit as a token of my honor to his memory. But as a Christian, I know his death has brought no "sting" to Ronald Reagan or his family. We can all be assured his soul rests in the presence of the God he knew, loved, and served so well here on earth.

My prayers for Mrs. Reagan are that the same Holy Spirit Who spoke to her husband, will comfort her. I pray also, He will open her spiritual ears to understand embryo stem cell research is an immoral activity, an affront to the Holiness of God. I pray before she dies, just like the lady in Rowe vs. Wade, Nancy will speak out against such activity.

For President Reagan's children, I pray each of you will have learned from the depth of your father's loving relationship with God, and reverence for following His ways. I pray you too will leave such a legacy to your children, and one day you will see your father again in Heaven.

In closing, I would like to thank God for giving me the ability to communicate this heart felt tribute to one of America's greatest Presidents. I have watched all week as so many glowing tributes came in from around the world. In each I could see pieces of the "Fruit of the Holy Spirit," which President Reagan made manifest in his life.

I thought to myself here was a man who like me, desired to show the image of God to others. As a Christian author I could never have found the right words to express my gratitude for his having met this goal so well in his life, had God not taught me how to value the same goal. I pray that in this tribute to both Ronald Reagan and the God he loved and served so faithfully, others will be inspired to seek that same goal in their life. May the people of America once again reflect the image of God to a cold, lost, lonely world.

Chapter Seven
JUSTICE IS A JOKE!
WHAT WE MUST DO TO SILENCE THE LAUGHTER

So often today it is said (and rightfully so), "Justice is a joke!"
In far too many instances it is a bad joke, as injustice seems destined to triumph over justice. I have heard it said, the reason why they call it the "criminal" justice system, is because it favors the "criminal." We need to change that idea and sick concept, by restoring justice, which extracts a fitting "punishment" upon the criminal. No more making excuses for their "unsocial" behavior. No more career criminals who get repeated hand slaps for doing something wrong. It's time justice once again had some REAL teeth, and not the FALSE teeth of whimpering liberals.

Some time ago in Tampa, two police officers were almost killed in an encounter with criminals. How outraged I and many others were, upon learning that these deadly criminals had a long (several pages) arrest record. Their last escapade had gotten them the same little "slap on the hand," house arrest (you stay home and be a good boy), which they had been given several times before. Was that effective? Just ask the police officers who had a gun battle with these jerks.

I was an assistant manager in a national drug store chain. Working the midnight shift in a dangerous neighborhood. It was a little after two A.M. and I had just let my cashier go on the first break of his shift. The only other person in the store was the pharmacist, who was on duty at the back of the store. When I was approached by what should have been two customers.

They asked me for three packs of cigarettes, which required turning my back on them to retrieve. Upon turning back with the cigarettes, using both hands, one held open the jean vest jacket he was wearing. He announced in a matter of fact manner, "If I have to take it out, I'll use it. Get the money out of the register and put it on the counter NOW!"

My reaction was calm, knowing I had the video camera focused perfectly on the scene. So I calmly asked, "What do you have?" In answer to my question, the bad guy opened the jacket, saying, "A 12 gage shotgun." Clearly in the lining of his jacket, was a sawed off 12 gage shotgun. I was thinking, "Got you dummy," as the camera had captured everything I could see. Popping the register open I replied with, "That's good enough for me."

The bad guy then made a request as I began to remove the cash from the register, "Would you put it in a bag please?" I felt like asking, "Paper or plastic?" But I knew these two brain dead people would not possess a sense of humor. So I just said, "You got it!" I watched, as the other bad guy, the one I call "the dummy," picked up a set of lighters and tossed them along with the cigarettes, into the bag. You could look into the eyes of "the dummy" and see drugs had destroyed whatever he may have had as a brain. He had the look expressed by Ross Parrot's VP when he was running for President. It said, "Who am I, and why am I here?" Bad guy #1 then announced, "We're leaving now, and if you stick your head out the door, I'll blow it off!" "Just get out of here!" was my reply.

Later, as the police detective and I were watching what I had captured so well on camera, I noticed a good thing. "Did you see that?" I very excitedly asked the detective. He asked me, "What?" I said, "The dummy put the lighters back!" We rewound the tape, and quickly found that the dummy had first picked up a set of the new on the market "Child guard" lighters, which were hard to get to light. Realizing how brain dead he was, the dummy put back the "child guard" lighters, and picked up a different set, those not having the "child guard" protection.

The detective walked with me to the counter and I pointed to the hook on which our friend "the dummy" had returned the lighter pack. He told the fingerprint guy to be sure to take fingerprints from that lighter pack. He did, and it helped them know who they were looking for. By the time all of the witnesses were called upon to identify the bad guys, they had done a total of 9 hold ups in the area. To the last one, each of us identified the actual criminals as the ones doing the crime. By the way, my video was flawless in offering clear identity of these two jerks.

After some time had passed, I received word they had been caught. Next came my having to be interviewed by a man from the state prosecutor's office. Also present, was an attorney who had been chosen to represent the bad guys. I told the DA, "The reason I asked to see the weapon was not because I am stupid. It was because I was counting on the bad guy being stupid (they always are – otherwise they would not be doing such STUPID things). I went on to say, in front of the defense attorney, "I did not want some liberal attorney getting them off by saying, "You didn't actually see a weapon, did you?" "I DID see a sawed off 12 gage shotgun in the lining of his jacket, just as the video shows." I watched, resisting the temptation of laughing, as the defense attorney made a frown.

When we had finished, I asked the DA if I might have a few minutes alone with him. The defense attorney went outside, and I made my point clear. I told him, "Florida has a mandatory seven year penalty for armed robbery. By my calculation, nine robberies, times seven, equals 63 years. I expect to see them get every one of those years. To this the DA replied, I don't think you'll be disappointed, we are asking for 25 years, and I don't believe we will have any trouble getting it."

Going to the door, and opening it to let myself out, I found the defense attorney kneeling at the peep hole. I felt so much like giving him a knee to the jaw, but as a Christian, I resisted the impulse. I decided I was going to like the trial, and give the defense lawyer a hard time defending two obviously guilty jerks.

WHAT TRIAL?

At last, the day of their trial came. I was excited and ready to go. I even arrived early, and waited and waited for my name to be called. When the time for the trial to begin had come and went, I decided it was time to find out what was going on. So I asked a clerk, and was told they had plea bargained, and there would be no trial. I was the only witness they had failed to contact and inform about this decision. I guess knowing my attitude about crime and punishment, they may have been afraid to contact me. "Would you like to have someone from the DA's office to come out and explain to you?" the lady asked. "I certainly WOULD!"

Shortly, an attorney from the DA's office who had been assigned this case came to speak with me. He started out apologetically saying, "I understand you were not informed the case had been plea bargained, and there will be no trial. I apologize for any inconvenience this may have caused you. I understand you have some questions for me?" "Yes, I do. First, I would like to know just why you had to "Plea Bargain" with these jerks. Every witness without doubt or exception identified them and my video clearly displayed the crime of armed robbery. So what was the need for a plea bargain?"

His answer was, "Well Mr. Callihan, it saved the state time and money to plea bargain. So when their attorney asked for a deal, we cut one." "May I ask just how many years did they get?" "Ten years" was his answer. I then asked boldly, "What happened to justice? Do you realize they did nine robberies here, and that's barely more than one year per robbery?"

In response he gave me a run down of what these guys had already been through in the justice system. He said they had been tried in Ohio for the car dealership, where after having just been released from prison, they had stolen a car and several blank tags. For this crime in Ohio, they had received a 25 year sentence. Then they had also received a 25 year sentence for the convenience store robbery they had committed in Missouri (again one robbery). Here in Florida, they had received ten years for nine robberies.

"Do you hear what you are telling me? In Ohio, they did one robbery, and received 25 years. In Missouri, they did one hold up, and received 25 years. But here, they did nine hold ups, and received a big 10 year sentence. Do you realize how stupid that sounds?" He said, "I don't think you have to worry about them, you and I will be long dead and buried before they ever see the light of day again." "Are you kidding, with the liberal morons we have in charge today, if they go one week without sneezing three times in a row, they release them, saying, now you go home and be a good boy. Your ten year sentence for nine robberies made a joke of justice!"

"I'm sorry you feel that way Mr. Callihan," he said. My reply was, "I'm sorry you have a job. Because it is obvious you are not interested in working for justice, nor to earn your pay." With that, I left feeling disgusted at what I had learned: forget the demands of justice, save time and money, go softly on the criminal. Is this what our laws and courts have mockingly become? I asked myself this as I was driving home.

I had known more of the history of these two criminals who had done the hold ups. I had found before engaging again in a life of crime in Ohio, here, and in Missouri, they had only recently been released from prison. What crime had they been guilty of committing which had landed them in prison? Armed robbery! Now here they were, recently released, going out and doing the same crime over again. Is this a sign of two VERY STUPID PEOPLE or what? Maybe so, but what about the STUPID disregard our justice system has for crime and punishing criminals?

I submit that We the People are the STUPID ones. Especially if we allow such a flawed system to continue malfunctioning as it currently is. We need to take back our court and justice system. How? I believe a good place to start, would be closing down the formerly "prestigious" schools, such as Harvard, Princeton, Yale, etc, etc. I am amazed and shocked that parents having the smarts to make enough money to pay the ridiculous asking price of these institutions of "ignorant learning," can't see what they are wasting their money on.

Do you really want your children to get an education from Communist professors who desire to see them come out hating and blaming America, mocking and making a joke of its system of justice? How can you have any brains, and send your child to where they might come out as an Obama, Holder, or Clinton? If you truly LOVE your children – why would you wish this upon them? I believe too many are sold on the old wife's tale: These are "prestigious" institutions of higher learning. No doubt at one time, long, long ago, this was so. However today evidence as provided by their graduates, indicated that has now become a stale and untrue tale.

If only the weakest links in our society sought an <u>education</u> for their children in these Communist infested, mentally and morally deficient places, we could see improvement. The Communist would have to go. These "so called" schools would fail and close due to lack of financing, if things don't change. We must wake up to the truth. The people in charge of many of our Colleges are a part of Khrushchev's plan and dream of taking us over from within, without ever having to fire a shot. Are we to continue sitting back, and allowing this to happen?

Another thing we might do, is DEMAND the power of RECALL and/or IMPEACHMENT of Judges, both Federal and Local. The ignorant decisions rendered by unfit judges, sometimes boggle the mind. Again I say, "We the People" are responsible for being Apathetic, and not demanding an effective means of RECORSE to address this issue.

Today, many judges sitting in courts (even the Supreme Court) have little or no fear (reverence) of the One True God, nor man. They believe since they are not answerable to "We the People," neither should they answer to a God in Whom they do not believe. "We the People" need to wake them up and shake them up to REALITY! Let's insist on making both Recall and Impeachment a viable tool in addressing unfit judges, and removing them from positions of authority.

I realize the lunatic liberal fringe is wildly screaming at me by now, trying their best to label me a nut case. Not so! I am simply a patriotic American, who is sick and tired of watching helplessly, as my country's freedoms are being flushed down the toilet. I am fed up! And I no longer will remain helpless. What about you? Will you join me, as the voice of "We the People" is LOUDLY heard again across our land?

When attending College, a course in Humanities was a required study. In taking Humanities, I learned a great lesson from history. ALL – without exception, of the former GREAT civilizations of the past, which are no longer around today, had one thing in common. I could see the common thread of APATHY, leading to their downfall. You could see corruption feeding from the bottom to the top. There was corruption of moral values, which eats away at a society like a cancer. There was instituted, a morally corrupt system of governing and of meeting out justice.

In spite of all of this evil being manifest, the motto of the people remained the same, "So what! We are still number one in the world!" This motto remained with them, as their APATHY carried them into being number zero in the world.

I ask. Will this become America's fate? Have we lost due to Apathy, our sense of patriotism? Can we find no worthy and REAL LEADERS to elect to positions of authority? Have all of the former STATESMEN and WOMEN, been replaced by two faced, spin – lying politicians?

America – One Nation Under Tyrants has been written by one seeking to awaken PATRIOTISM in the hearts of America's men and women once more. It is a call to come out of APATHY and take back our country from the heathen! I will be the first to admit, it is not a book for the feeble hearted to read. They might have a heart attack. It is for those who still love America, and have a rightful reverence for the One True God, under Whose guidance America was founded.

What if you are of a "Religion"? That's O.K., you can still LOVE AMERICA, at least enough to do something to stop its demise into the garbage heap of history! I wish to see justice and leadership which have our Best Interest – restored among "We the People." I desire this for every American, whether you have "Religion" with a false god, or share the "Relationship" of a child, son, or daughter, of the One True God.

Chapter Eight
AS CHRISTIANS WE KNOW A BETTER WAY

Recently, I received an e-mail notice informing me that Disney World would be putting on its celebration of "Gay" day. It would occur on a first Saturday in June, during regular park hours. At this "event," would be homosexuals, transvestites, and other demon possessed people suffering from perverted ideas of what sex is about.

The Christian group informing of this, asked if I would send an e-mail of protest to the executives at Disney. I was more than happy to do so, as I believe they are a disgrace to the memory of Mr. Disney. As a "Baby Boomer," while growing up, Mr. Walt Disney was a man who loved children. In the world of Hollywood, where many corrupt and immoral ideas were being pushed on America's youth by an industry caring only for money, Mr. Disney was a bright exception.

He truly cared for the moral values, we as Americans might grow up attaining. As the result, his movies and cartoons were always interesting, entertaining and filled with moral decency of a very high caliber. To say he was a man of moral backbone would be a vast understatement. Mr. Disney was always willing to take stands on moral issues, which others had neither the will nor courage to take. My youth, as well as countless others, was morally enriched by the quality Mr. Disney stood for. He was almost like a guardian angel to kids of all ages. How I miss that man. I am certain he is in Heaven. How America needs many like him, especially today!

The sad news about the request I received from a Christian organization, was their eagerness of finding a way to appease the execs at Disney. Wishing to keep everybody happy, and allowing Disney to save face; they suggested the "event" be held "after" regular park hours. At least this way, innocent families who had brought their children to Disney World, would not have to suffer through immoral and abhorrent behavior, being shoved down their throat. The goals of that being, to make the idea of perverted behavior become labeled simply, an "alternate" lifestyle.

As part of this appeasement, it was pointed out that events such as Christians' Night of Joy, is always scheduled after the park has officially closed; thereby separating the Christians from any whose soul might be in need of salvation. God forbid such an offensive thing, as someone becoming "born again" by the Spirit of the Living and One True God. Yet offer for the whole world to see – the sick, perverted, and demonic actions of those who are deceived by satan!

May I say, I had enough! I made no offer of appeasement. I rather strongly suggested they cancel the entire "event," as it is of disgrace to the memory of Walt Disney. He deserves better than a bunch of immoral morons deciding on what will make money, over what is morally responsible and the morally correct thing to do. Will they take my suggestion seriously? That remains to be seen. Today, so many sacrifice their morals on the alter of "political correctness," selling their immortal soul for money.

"Political Correctness," is just a flimsy excuse many use for choosing to sell their soul to satan, following his ways, rather than God's. When I see spineless wimps offering this as an excuse for their lack of moral backbone, it makes me SICK! Especially when the one doing so, is a religious person attempting to wear the label "Christian" (A follower of Christ). Such people are only deceiving themselves, not God, nor "Relationship" Christians.

Who and what are "Relationship" Christians? They are those who in having become born again by the Spirit of God, choose to bring honor and glory to their Father in Heaven, by walking in the Spirit, and dwelling within the Kingdom of God each day. They share the Loving Relationship with their Father in Heaven. The Relationship – not Religion, which Jesus came to restore between God and mankind. They know the secret of how to do as God's Word tells us to do – "Be Holy, as your Father in Heaven is Holy."

They accomplish this seemingly impossible request, by choosing to each day, die to self, yielding their will (their spirit) to the guidance of God's will (His HOLY Spirit). They choose wisely, to be guided ONLY by the Spirit of Truth, Who lives and reigns within their heart. They are not mindless followers of the doctrines, dogmas, and traditions of man-made "Religion." They take what is spoken in John 1:12 (KING JAMES VERSION – not any of the Watered Down versions), they seek to use the Power they have been given by Jesus, to grow up – to become the Spiritually Mature son or daughter of God, which God created us to become. How do you do this? Please check out what it says in Romans 1:14. They understand the FULL meaning of what Romans 1:8 says; not stopping at the comma!

But lets get down to looking at the subject of this chapter, the Better Way we as Christians have of effectively helping the spiritually challenged make wise moral decisions. Today, we see in the "entertainment" business and other forms of distraction, the name of Jesus, out Lord, God, and Savior, being sickly maligned by those who do not know Him. How many calling themselves "Christian" support this through choosing to buying the sponsors products? How many sit in apathy, wishing that "they" (the entertainment business) would not promote immorality?

We know from previous examples, the name "Mohammed" is NOT to be treated with disrespect. Why? Because fear of reprisals from his fanatical followers, keeps the creeps from offending that guy. Not so with Christians! We are taught to Love our enemy, do good to those who use and abuse us, showing forgiveness, patience, and kindness instead. Why are we to treat offenders in this way? So that they may know we are children of our Father in Heaven. Those making threats of barbaric behavior, are in service to their father, only his home is not Heaven.

We can help the spiritually challenged make sound moral decisions, through loving them enough to protest, taking a firm and strong stand against their disregard of God and His Ways of Holiness. We may most effectively protest, by writing them intelligent, not physically threatening letters, speaking out against moral decay. We may help, by insisting they take a stand against such moral decay. In doing so, we clearly may threaten not to purchase their product(s) –MEANING EXACTLY WHAT WE SAY! If you hit them in their pocketbook, it will force them to make much wiser decisions, regarding what they can and cannot push off on people.

In the 1950's when I was growing up, parents had moral backbone, and the guts to not go for any idiotic idea such as "Political Correctness." Stores selling demonic and immoral music to their children, would have become boycotted out of business. Disney World would have had trouble attracting families to their parks, had they held such an abomination as "Gay Night." Business owners knew this was so, as the result they were very careful about what they chose to sell.

My question to the parents of today is: Have you become so corrupted by interest in "Self" and by "Apathy," that you lack the guts to take a stand for the good of not only your children, but those of others whose parents indeed are pathetically into Self and Apathy? My question to those calling themself "Christian is: Are you just an empty, powerless, "religious" label wearer, lacking the guidance of God's Holy Spirit; or the willingness to be guided by Him?

Those brave men and women who founded America, were not the least lacking in moral backbone. Their greatest hope was for America to be a country of people desiring to bring honor and glory to the ONE TRUE GOD! The precious freedoms we have known for so many years, were due to this goal which they had in their heart, while building America. Today it is sad to see how perilously close we are to loosing our freedoms one by one. We also are so dangerously close to loosing God's hand of Providence. The events of the nut case who tried to explode a bomb, by burning his crotch; and the other nut who failed to set off the car bomb in New York, were called "Lucky" events by those politicians who do not know the One True God. What a Sick bunch of CLOWNS are representing the will of "We the people"!

We as Christians, know and have a better way of helping the spiritually challenged pay attention to moral ideals. May God give us another Walt Disney, is my prayer. Kids are being short changed by the "entertainment" business of today. This is true not only in America, but around the world. Have you heard about the SICK television program put out by Hamas? A cartoon show, where Israelis are portrayed to children, as being less than human. How sad that Hamas also is lacking a Walt Disney among their population!

Chapter Nine
THE LESSONS FROM 2008
BEFORE YOU VOTE – COUNT THE COST!

There are valuable lessons to be learned from the election of 2008. However, only those caring enough about preserving the greatness of America will be earnest in learning from them. So many callous and unnecessary mistakes were made by voters in 2008. One must look introspectively to discover where the blame lies.

The debacle we now are forced to call "president" Obama, came about through voters who were not cautious in whom they chose voting for. They failed to count the cost by closely examining the evidence candidate Obama was putting forth each day. There was overwhelming evidence of a man who was not capable of the job, a man who was greatly lacking moral backbone and fiber, and one having disdain for the American way of life. Blatantly he displayed these truths, in both words and actions. So many voters seemed uninterested. Unfortunately now we are paying the cost for their lack of caring, and what a great price it is!

What are Obama's disqualifications? To give only a few examples: refusal to wear an American flag pin, or not holding his hand over his heart while **not** saying the pledge of allegiance to the flag. To the uneducated, these seemingly "small" signs are actually BIG signs of one lacking a Patriotic heart for America. How about moral backbone? What moral backbone??? This poor man openly admitted he was not being paid enough to know if the murder of innocent babies in their mother's womb for convenience was a moral or immoral thing. The answer is not about PAY! It is about possessing the moral backbone to do the right thing for fellow human beings, namely those defenseless and innocent little babies.

Can we ever forget, or offer enough thanks to "Joe the Plumber"? Now famous for having prompted the truth to come from Obama's mouth, regarding his plans to "spread the wealth." Though many laughed, and some thought of a modern day "Robin Hood," who would rob from "The Rich" and give to "The Poor." Yet 100 years earlier, the same sentiments were touted in Russia, using the phrase: **"Down with the Bourgeoisie!"** Bourgeoisie refers to "The Rich" in Russian. How few understood, or even grasped the real intent of "spreading the wealth"? One might ask, how can history repeat itself? Easy, if our colleges never bother to teach about the use of the term, "Down with the **Bourgeoisie**" (The Rich) during the Communist revolution. Keep the students dumb and uninformed, and it's easier to make dupes of them!

How few cared to protect America from Communism, by denying control of the Presidency and Congress to one party, the American Communist Party? Now, because so few bothered to count the cost, America is on the edge of becoming a Communist system. Our government is full of people in positions of power, who hate our freedoms and way of life. They are spending us into bankruptcy, with the goal of seeing America fall as a great nation. Worse of all, they are doing these things through the apathetic complacency of voters who just don't care enough to understand what is at stake. I reiterate, if there is one very important lesson "We the people" can learn from 2008, it is we desperately need a "NO CONFIDENCE VOTE!"

When "We the people," accidentally elect incompetent persons as leaders, they should not be given a full term to work their destruction on America. "We the people," who by our vote hired them, should have the right to say, as does Donald Trump, "You're FIRED! Only say it LOUDLY, and with more GUSTO than has ever been heard! We really must insist on this vital **RIGHT**, to preserve us from the blunder of 2008 ever happening again.

The military taught very effectively about a totalitarian form of government. The only Rights you have are the ones you are told you have. The only Freedoms you have are those granted to you by your "Superiors" (who sometimes are not superior in intelligence to a grasshopper). The goals you are willing to fight and die for, are the ones prescribed to you by your military leaders. A good example would be the gathering of "body counts" ordered during the Vietnam War. Officers would order soldiers to go out onto the battlefield (sometimes while the battle was not yet over) and count the bodies of the dead. This was how they determined if we had won or lost a battle – by the number of the enemy dead, as opposed to our dead. Many soldier lost their life, while attempting to get "body counts."

In the America I grew up in, our Freedoms were given to all Americans, regardless of their "Religious" beliefs. However, our Freedoms, unlike other countries, are granted to us by the Providence of the One True God. They are guaranteed by our government (those whom "We the people" put into office). Our Freedoms are not to be infringed upon by an oppressive government. This is due to a foundation document called our Constitution. Upon this document, the powers and limitations of our government are clearly defined.

Concepts such as our Liberty and Independence are also based in our ability of worshiping and serving the One True God. This is why we are so close to loosing both today, so few understand this vital fact. Who do you think has protected America from attack during our past conflicts? History tells us it wasn't Buddha, Mohammed, or some other mystical god. It was the One True God, to whom most Americans of our past, worshipped, served, and prayed to when in battle!

But what kind of legacy are we leaving today? Do we really want our children and their children deriving their "Rights" from the government, rather than the One True God? Do we desire to see the Constitution trashed by an oppressive government, or by "Supremes" who have a disdain for honoring the One True God, while gladly defending the false gods of satan and man? Is it your goal to see concepts of Liberty and Independence disappear from the shores of America? If it is, take warning. I and other Americans are willing to kick your butt off of America's shores!

I realize some readers may feel very offended by what I have spoken in this book. But I long to see the America which recognized, honored, and sought to serve and share a relationship with the One True God, more than the empty headed false gods of satan and man. The One True God is a God of Love, because He created you and me to be His children, who hopefully will make the effort through receiving His Son, Jesus, and His Holy Spirit, to become His spiritually mature sons and daughters. He is our Loving Dad!

You may wish for America to be under the god of death, despair, hatred, and darkness. You may desire for America to be under the thousands of phony little gods of Buddhism. You even may want America to have no God at all – especially the One True GOD! But too bad! America was founded as a nation to be under the Providence and Guidance of the One TRUE GOD! Sure, we offer you "religious tolerance" – unlike what your god would offer. But we refuse to allow the True God in Whom we place our Trust, to be undermined by your phony god. We do not hate you, only the deception satan has worked in your mind, to keep you from knowing your Father in Heaven, and how much He loves you. We will never bow to or serve false gods, but we gladly will offer to lovingly teach you about the One True God; Who is a God of Love, Light, and Abundant Life.

In closing this chapter, I must make note of the fact that the voters in 2008 had very poor choice of leadership to vote for. Indeed, John Mc Cain is more of a TRUE War hero, than the band-aid wearing John Kerry ever was or will be. However, I view Mc Cain as another Alan Specter. I never forgot all of the times his vote in the Senate helped the Democrats make the operative word, "Gridlock" work against President George Bush, the 1st. Gridlock was used to keep effective legislation from being passed. It was the pressure applied by the Democrats, to make President Bush go back on his word, and raise taxes, as the Demos demanded him to do. Falsely, they promised to lift

"Gridlock," if President Bush would raise taxes on the people. He was naïve, and trusted them to be honorable. But to no avail. Mc Cain voted so many times with the Democrats, keeping important legislation from seeing the light of day.

Personally, I was not thrilled that a two faced politician was the only other alternate choice to vote for, rather than an avowed Communist. But at least Mc Cain had two things going in his favor. His wise choice of a running mate and his ability to have the intelligence to know the murder of an innocent baby in its mother's womb is immoral, and needs to be stopped. He did not request higher PAY, to make this decision. This alone, proved he had greater moral backbone than Obama.

IF (and that's a BIG IF) we survive the debacle of 2008, it will only be by the Grace of the One True God. If we are willing to pray, and are given another chance, let's not waste it! First, we must DEMAND from Congress, the right to hold NO CONFIDENCE votes on ALL political offices and appointed judgeships. This will offer us further protection against falling into the hands of a tyrant. Why should fools have four years or less, to destroy our way of life? WE HIRE – WE CAN FIRE! This is the slogan I propose we use. Secondly, let us end the process of having to vote for the lesser of two evils. Can we not find intelligent, God fearing men and women to elect to positions of leadership? Are such days gone forever? I pray they are not!

If we survive until 2012, let our voting public learn from the 2008 debacle. It is important to count the cost, before voting for unworthy and unqualified buffoons to represent us as President and Vice-president. We need strong, vibrant, and God fearing men and women, to lead us back to prosperity and strength among the nations of the world. We need people with moral backbones, who are willing to stand up against morally corrupt practices (Socialism and Communism being among them).

Lastly, if the writings in this book sound too "preachy" for you, you have my sympathy. You just don't get it! 2008 has failed to give you an education. You enjoy staying blissfully IGNORANT! I believe America will survive. Why? Because the majority of Americans have learned from the lessons 2008 has taught us. They GET IT! Let the Ignorant stay Ignorant, the majority of voters this fall and in 2012, will be Intelligent. No longer will they fail to count the cost of electing jerks to positions of authority.

Do I sound like an angry Republican? Perhaps! But in effect and actuality, I am simply an angry American, who is tired of daily watching the efforts being made to destroy the country I love and grew up in. That's A FACT JACK!

Chapter Ten
HIS DREAM CAME TRUE

In the early 1960's, Nikita Khrushchev issued a bold threat to Americans. "We will bury you without firing a shot!" At the time many Americans took his threat lightly, a blusterous remark made by a Communist dictator. How few realized he was speaking about a master plan developed by minds in service to satan.

Today as I am writing, many never heard of his threat. It is never mentioned in History classes. Some don't remember due to loss of memory. Then there are those who do remember, yet believe his threat was and is just a joke. But sadly, today as I am writing, I have lived to see, and am witnessing his dream coming true in America.

In the early 1960's, I once got to see a documentary in a movie theatre. Today most likely it would not be allowed to run in America's theatres. In it was an expose' on just how Khrushchev and the Communist Party planned on executing the take over of America. It was through a little known or recognized weakness called – EDUCATION. That, combined with our respect for "freedom of speech," would eventually be the areas of attack which could lead to our downfall.

The documentary showed how in Russia, students from grade school age up were being taught to become a good "facsimiles" of American youth. They were being taught to speak without an accent, know the latest slang words, modes of dress and dances. Then they were to be imported into the U.S., growing up attending our high schools, colleges, and universities, receiving degrees as teachers, lawyers, and media reporters. Those in teaching were to establish a foothold in the education industry, gaining tenure as teachers in American schools.

As they established positions of authority, they were to hire more of their compatriots into our school system. Those who gained the status of attorney were to seek appointment as judges. Then they were to use their position to undermine any and every moral value upon which America's foundation had been built. They were to work also at getting into politics, running for Congress, and eventually the Presidency itself. Such a plan takes a great deal of time to come to fruition, But looking at the victory and great prize to be gained, the Communists were willing to play the waiting game. Those in the media were to twist truth to fit their form of indoctrination and propaganda.

It has taken over fifty years for Khrushchev's plan and dream to come true. Most likely he is now rolling over in his grave with laughter at how easily the Americans have been duped! Just look at the condition of our education system today. I have often said, our kids are sent off to college to become educated morons, just like their teachers. However, I must admit my comment is off center to what really is happening. In reality our kids are being indoctrinated to become ignorant Communists, as they are being taught to hate America and all of her morals and ideals. They are being told the rest of the world doesn't envy us – they hate us for our ideals. They are being taught America's foundation is old, crumbling, and needing "change" (hum, does that word sound vaguely familiar?).

The Democratic Party, once a viable party of people having a love for America, long ago became taken over by the American Communist Party. Yes, you who are blissfully ignorant and naïve may laugh at me for stating this fact. But to the intelligent among us the facts speak for themselves! Just watch as our freedoms crumble over the next three years – try laughing about that!

Our institutions for higher education have become so taken over by Communism, it's actually difficult to get an intelligent teacher hired, especially an intelligent Christian teacher. Parents are blindly willing to pay big money to see their children come out not just "educated morons," but as well indoctrinated Communists dupes. The 2008 election proves Khrushchev and his gang have finally won. Their brilliant plan has succeeded in placing America into the incapable hands of the American Communist Party.

Communism hates Christianity. Because they know Christianity is the biggest threat to their atheistic view of the world. Lies and liars always fear the truth, for it undermines their beliefs in and efforts to push a false reality.

How many are going to sit back in apathy and watch as freedom of speech comes under attack in our Congress and our court system? Obama declared in his campaign that America no longer is a Christian nation. As President, he now brags about this in every foreign country he visits. Votes which he received from "Christian label wearers" prove his assumption to be correct.

What are we to do? I for one owe many an apology. In my patriotic love affair with America, which has been ongoing for over sixty six years now, I have on occasion, called those who voted for Obama and the American Communist Party (Democrats), fools. I spoke in anger, as an enraged Patriot who hates to watch helplessly as his country is being murdered. In retrospect, I have come to realize that "fool" is far too harsh a word to have used. For all who may have taken offense at my bad choice of wording, I issue a sincere apology.

Looking upon what really happened, I realize now that it was the ignorant, duped, immature, gullible and naive among us that callously voted to put the American Communists Party into a position of authority. A bag of hot air,

Nikita's "Dream Child," has now attained the position of President, not of the United States, but of the new Socialist Republic of America (SRA). Am I despondent over this? No way! I am merely disappointed that for decades we have watched in apathy, as our system of government was being eroded and attacked from within. I am appalled so few Patriots seem to remain alive in America. Even more, how few true Christians exist, those honoring God and His ways of holiness. Such a Christian would never have voted for one boasting of his stand on abortion and homosexual marriage.

The premise of this book evokes the question: Is there still hope for America? My answer would be as long as God is still on His throne, and there is a remnant of Christians, there is hope. I mean Christians who are unafraid to work as harvesters in the field to deliver those enslaved by ignorance, into knowledge of the Truth concerning God's will and ways. The early Americans had a love for both God's will and ways. In fact, they proved their love by seeking His guidance and ways in establishing the foundation of our freedoms. They desired a country where they, and generations to come, could be free to love and serve the One **True** God, without fear of suppression, oppression, or physical suffering for it.

Perhaps the greatest exploited weakness in our freedoms satan has used to destroy us is the use of the word "RELIGION" when describing freedom. That one little word opened the door to any and all of satan's demonic practices and false gods. It also gives covering to man's imagination, which rejects the One True God, and replaces Him with fictitious gods.

Listen! If the Communists can establish a foothold in America, so can we as Christians! If we allow them to have a strangle hold, it may prove a little more difficult, yet still do-able. What we need is for men and women who are truly committed **Christians** to run for political office, and gain positions of authority and judgeship. We need true Christian people to invade our institutions of higher education, and work to take back our school system. What we as Christians need to do is be willing to back and support those Christians who are brave enough and patriotic enough to get involved in winning America back to serving the One True God. No more label wearer only, ignorant, "Lukewarm," or naive Christian voters! Become intelligent; seek out information as to what candidates truly believe; and where candidates actually stand on important issues. If their stand is against the moral laws of God – DON'T VOTE FOR OR IN ANY WAY SUPPORT THEM!

Had this happened in 2008 we may not be where we are today. My call is not for the feeble hearted. It is for the patriotic, those who feel America has been betrayed, yet still seek for God to keep His hand of Providence upon us, as we battle to regain what we have lost. We owe this service not just to God, but also to our founding fathers. Remember, they risked all they had, home and even life, to give us the greatest of countries ever established on earth. Are we to just sit by in apathy, watching, as satan and his demonically possessed destroy it?

My call is for Americans to join me in praying for Barry Obama and his family to receive a Damascus road experience with God. Oh that Jesus Himself would educate the Obama family to know He is REAL, not just a name to throw around to deceive and get votes from the naive and ignorant. That Jesus would make him painfully aware of the sanctity of innocent little lives he so callously would seek to destroy; that the Holiness of God would make him fear endorsing immoral practices. Lastly, that the LOVE of God, would touch both the Obama's and Henry Wright, that they might come into the Kingdom of God, and reject the hatred found in the world.

My prayer encompasses far more than just the Obama family. I pray God would use RELATIONSHIP Christians to help all who voted for Obama, to have their spiritual eyes and ears opened to the truth. We can do this best by example. I must confess, mine has been a poor one, as I have in anger called many a fool. I deeply regret that, as it was wrong. It's not too late for you who are Relationship – not Religious Christians reading this book. Please go out and do what my burst of anger has perhaps made me incapable of doing, help bring people into the knowledge of and Light of the Truth; the truth about both God and America's foundation.

Saint Paul tells us, "Some of you were once thieves, prostitutes, **immoral politicians**, **unjust judges**, **Godless reporters**, **teachers of perversion**, and **lying lawyers**. But now you have been sanctified by the blood of the Lamb; now you have become born again by the Spirit of Truth." I am a poor one to judge others. But I am one to encourage others to bring their fellow Americans to the knowledge of the Truth, concerning the One True God – under Whose authority America was created to be governed by. Will you commit to doing this? Do it, not just for me, nor just for God, but for the survival and reemergence of America as once more a GREAT NATION among the nations in the world.

By the way, let's put In GOD We Trust **BOLDLY** back on our money, in a place of prominence. This is the path to revival and economic survival for America! Printing trillions of dollars, without the Love of God and His righteousness in the hearts of America's people, is useless! Sorry to have to be the one to tell you – but it's true!

Chapter Eleven
WILL HIS NIGHTMARE COME TRUE?

In 1963, having graduated from high school I took a summer job working for a television repair man. Mr. Andy Anderson, owner of A to Z television repair, gave me my very first legitimate real paying job. I was so thrilled, yet a bit scared by some of the situations I found myself in.

As a child, like most boys I would climb about anything and everything. That is until I took a very bad fall, breaking open my knee cap. I had climbed up a tree and fallen to hit a manhole cover. It was grated with those raised points. They tore my knee cap off, it was hanging by a small piece of flesh, and I was bleeding profusely. Mary Smith, a neighbor having training as a nurse, cleaned the area and patched me up. She wrapped my knee very tightly and did an outstanding job. I have only a small scar on my knee cap.

Nevertheless, this incident made me loose my confidence in my climbing ability, and my ability to keep my balance. I developed vertigo, a fear of heights. When I discovered that some of the requirements of my job would be to climb high on a ladder to help put an antenna on a roof top, or attach one to a chimney, I was never comfortable. A lot of prayers went up to God, asking for my guardian angel to have good balance. Andy was very patient with me, as it would take me a long time to climb up and even longer to climb down.

This is the background for what happened that unforgettable summer. One day we were called to a home in South St. Pete. A lady came to the door and invited us to come in. As we entered the living room, a man appearing elderly was in a sort of wheelchair. He was having problems with the remote control to his garage door opener. We were invited to sit with him as Andy went to work on the remote device.

At once, Mr. Anderson introduced the man to me. He said, "Joe, this is Doctor Robert Oppenheimer." I responded with the usual, "It's very nice to meet you sir." Seeing I seemed to be unimpressed, Andy then asked, "Do you know who Doctor Oppenheimer is?" As I could not remember hearing of or going to a local Doctor named Oppenheimer, I said an honest, "No, I'm afraid I don't."

With a big grin on his face Mr. Anderson announced, "Dr. Oppenheimer is the Father of the Atomic bomb." At once I remembered having heard that name. It was in my high school history class. WOW I thought! I am in the presence of a man who changed the history of mankind.

Doctor Oppenheimer's wife fixed a nice lunch for Mr. Anderson and me. As Mr. Anderson was busy working on the remote, I took advantage of this opportunity to speak with this man of historic importance. I began by telling him what an impact his invention had on World War II. I told him, "You saved many lives on both sides by bringing the war to a quick end."

His reply kind of surprised me. Doctor Oppenheimer said he was not so sure his invention was a blessing to mankind, but more of a curse. Wanting to reassure him I responded by saying, "Your invention has helped make war an idiotic idea, as there can be no more victors – only losers." To this, Doctor Oppenheimer said, he felt betrayed by America.

I guess he could see the look of shock in my eyes at this remark, so he explained what had prompted such an attitude. Doctor Oppenheimer said, "I was promised by our government, this would be the most carefully guarded secret, since the entrance to the Garden of Eden. I was assured no other nation would ever gain access to this secret weapon." He went on to lament, "It took no time at all for the Rosenberg's to give it away to Russia. The great care I had been promised did not exist."

Doctor Oppenheimer went on to tell me of his sleepless nights. He said, "I can tell you I have had many sleepless nights, filled with nightmares of what some future generation may be facing one day." His story still rings in my ears today, as I ask of you the reader, how close are we to seeing his nightmares come true? Only God knows the answer. As a nation are we closer or farther away from God since the early 1960's? Do we still deserve God's hand of protection upon us?

You can imagine my indignation, when several years after the death of Doctor Oppenheimer and his wife, I found a movie playing on television. It was about the birth of the atomic bomb. In it was liberal Hollywood's attempt to bring Dr. Oppenheimer over to their flawed point of view. I got disgusted as I watched the person playing Dr. Oppenheimer, making an impassioned plea to release knowledge of the atomic bomb to Russia and other countries of the world. Following the usual liberal lie, his supposed motive was to "insure" world "peace."

What an OUTRAGEOUS LIE! Being the cowards they are, Hollywood had waited until long after the death of Dr. Oppenheimer and his wife, to attempt putting such words into his mouth. Had he been alive, I feel sure the man I spoke with briefly in 1963, would not only have told Hollywood to go to Hell; he would have sued the Hell out of them for SLANDER!

You see, having met and heard him in his own words, I know of this man's heart. But those who never got to meet him personally, and those born after his time, know only fictitious lies put out by the liberal nuts in Hollywood. Sadly, once there was an era when Hollywood put out quality, truthful, **entertainment**. It was not as yet run by a group of Communists, whose goal is to use films to indoctrinate and persuade the gullible into believing in their way of life.

I dare to ask, are we really choosing to honor and serve the One True God? As a people who allow the expulsion of the One True God from our schools, removal of His Ten Commandments from courtrooms so they will not **offend** lying lawyers, defendants, complainants, and witnesses; refusing to allow prayer to the One True God, but happily kissing the behind of satan's false gods; what do we as a nation say? Sadly the answer is a no brainer! Having turned our country's government over to the American Communist Party, filled with immoral God hating people, I dare to ask, does God have any obligation to protect us from such a nightmare coming to pass?

Does the answer to such questions make you feel as if our future looks bleak? It does indeed look bleak. But only if we stay in a condition of **apathy** regarding taking back our country from the heathens. The One TRUE God is the ONLY One Who can keep America safe, Just as He did through two World Wars, Korea, Viet Nam, Iraq, and Afghanistan. If you care about America, your future, and that of your children, grandchildren, or other children - WAKE UP! COME OUT OF YOUR APATHY!

What can you do? Are you capable of running for a position of authority in our government, or legal system? Are you a teacher who has been running in fear of the heathens? Remember when Christians used to be in charge of our school systems? The Communists had no fear of them. They had a legal system which they had polluted with unjust judges to issue immoral judgments in their favor. If they can do this, why not turn it around? Why can't we do the same (using people of a moral backbone) in reclaiming our country? Why should we fear immoral people? Do they have the One True God on their side? NO! They have only dumb little satan!

We are nearing the close of this book. Its purpose has not been to inspire depression. It has exposed the sad truth regarding the decline of a once great nation. But it has encouraged True Christians (those having The One True God on their side) to seek God's help to raise America from the ashes, to once more become GREAT among the nations of the world! This can be done. It is achievable, just as Nikita's evil plan was.

With God as our Master Planner we cannot fail - if we are diligent, and remain diligent in not only securing our freedoms again, but protecting them from the evil within. Our founding fathers relied on the One True God to guide them. Their faith in Him was not flimsy. In their day, satan never would have gotten abortion and other immoral practices to be acceptable. They would never have bought into the - it's only an "alternate lifestyle" argument. They knew what God calls an abomination before Him, IS – an ABOMINATION before A Holy God!

Religion has blinded the Spiritual eyes of so many calling themselves a <u>Christian</u>. The cries of God's Spirit, which are heard in the writing of this book, are not for the lukewarm. Those interested in meeting Jesus in the clouds upon His return, will listen and take this warning to heart. God says in His Word, He needs only a <u>dedicated,</u> **diligent** "remnant," to accomplish great things. Are you one of them? If so, let God inspire you to greatness by His Holy Spirit. Then you go out and inspire others to take back our great country, which was and is dedicated to be under the wisdom, providence, and control – not of false gods – but of the One TRUE God?

If you don't do this we are destined to become like the poor people living in Iran. Under the leadership of "Religious Fanatics" who <u>force</u> upon all, worship of, and service to, satan's false god. Not a God of infinite love for the heathen; but a god of bitter hatred toward all "infidels." Is this the kind of tyrannical god you desire to see "we the people" being forced to bow down to worship and serve?

Will such a thing come to pass? We are already so close, and why? Because of the apathy which says, "Let someone else do it." The kind of apathy which permits you to be comfortable casting your vote for immoral jerks (putting it as <u>politely</u> as I can). How irresponsible? Voting for those who desire to vanquish and destroy everything giving praise, honor, and glory, to the One True God.

Where do you stand today, in this time of crisis? Are you among the puny, gutless wonders, supporting immoral jerks? Or are you just a bag of wind, loud, but not having the guts to stand up and make a difference? Or, could you be the leader God is seeking to help raise up, and work to reclaim our nation for Him? I pray you are among the last group. God and America need for you to stand up, speak out, and make the kind of difference needed to turn America back to following the One True God!

Chapter Twelve
IS AMERICA LOSING OUR "IN" DEPENDENCE?

Over two hundred years ago, America's founding fathers signed a document proudly proclaiming our "Declaration of Independence."
It was to clarify the fact that the Colonists no longer would tolerate being overtaxed by England. Freedom became the rallying cry of patriots. Americans were willing to risk everything including their life in order to create the most unusual nation in the history of man, one offering freedom to worship the One True God, not the false gods of satan and man's "religions."
satan's ability to use the word "Religion" as acceptable to man left open the door for the state of confusion America is in today. Jesus, Son of the One True God, did not come to earth to establish yet another "Religion." There was already enough of that garbage around on the earth when He arrived. Jesus came to restore our "Relationship" with the One True God. The relationship which Adam and Eve had lost by following satan into sin.
During the Civil War, as brother was put into a position of fighting against brother, both sides believed God was in their favor. According to the fact sheet published by the Department of the Treasury, then Treasury Secretary, Salom P. Chase received many appeals from devout persons throughout the country, urging that the United States recognize "the Deity" (Which the majority of Americans recognized as the "One True God") on U.S. coins.
As the result, Secretary Chase instructed James Pollock, Director of the Mint at Philadelphia, to prepare a motto, in a letter dated November 20, 1861. The following is what Secretary Chase said:
"Dear Sir, No nation can be strong except in the strength of God, or safe except in His defense. The TRUST of our people in GOD should be declared on our national coins.
Will you cause a device to be prepared without unnecessary delay, with a motto expressing in the fewest and tersest words possible this national recognition?"
In December of 1863, the Director of the Mint submitted designs. He proposed using either, OUR COUNTRY, OUR GOD or OUR GOD, OUR TRUST. In a letter submitted to the Mint Director on December 9, 1863, Secretary Chase stated:
"I approve your mottos, only suggesting that on that with the Washington obverse the motto should begin with the word OUR, so as to read OUR GOD AND OUR COUNTRY. And on that with the shield, it should be changed so as to read IN GOD WE TRUST."

Congress passed the Act of April 22, 1864. In 1864 the motto, IN GOD WE TRUST first appeared on the two cent coin. Later, a law passed by the 84th Congress and approved by the President on July 30, 1956. It declared: IN GOD WE TRUST is to be the national motto of the United States of America.

Have you noticed something REAL about this history? Our money and our motto do not state: "In the Deity" we trust. They also do not say: "In the "unknown god" We Trust." Please tell me, where they say: "In mohammed, buddha, obama, or willie - We Trust?"

Have you ever wondered why this is so? Because the majority of Americans understood, placing your trust in ANY other god than the One True God, ALL HOPE is thrown out the window. False gods of satan and of man's imagination have no authority to offer Providence toward a people. Being empty and powerless, they cannot deliver strength, protection, and prosperity. Americans in the 1800's and 1950's had not become so full of Religion (as those of today), they no longer recognized Who the One True God IS!

He IS the One we address as **Our Father**, in our prayers to Him. To the Religious crowd, He is The Man Upstairs, or The Man in the Sky, or The Supreme Being. To the atheist, mistakenly, He is the non-existent. Although looking at the universes and observing order not chaos; the Heavens declare belief in a non-existent God, to be that of only a fool.

But what of the initial decision of putting In God We Trust on our money? Americans realizing that the very Union which had been entrusted to their care, was in danger of being destroyed, turned with Faith to make a declaration of IN Whom we DEPEND on to keep America United and Strong – THE ONE TRUE GOD!

After having obtained victory in both World Wars I and II, Americans desired for the whole world to know: In the One True God is our Dependence to be found. So, In God We Trust was adopted as our national motto. What a Country! A nation of Light and Hope! Like a magnet America drew people of other countries to her shores.

But just look at the America of today, because of that one little word, "Religion," belief on the One True God is being put down; while satan and man's false – empty headed gods, are being raised up. This prompts me to ask: Are we in danger of losing our IN (The One True God) DEPENDENCE? It is clear, the sad answer is yes. Today many are pushing belief in satan's false, and man's goofy gods, to be the "replacement" for the One True God in America.

Where are Christian voices of protest? The label wearing, powerless religious "Christians," are sitting by in silent Apathy! They quickly run away in fear, the moment the words "Religious Freedom" are used to silence protest of false gods trying to take over life in American. Because their faith is misplaced, they are gutless and powerless. They relay on the teachings of twisted scriptures by modern day Pharisees, to instruct them "about" the one they believe is God, but they never get to <u>know</u> Him as Dad.

Religion fears the Spirit of Truth, the Holy Spirit of God. For all who trust in and seek His guidance, He will lead into All Truth. Religion's dark lies, deceptions, and lack of power are exposed by the Light of Truth. With their spiritual eyes opened, in seeing the Truth - religion's followers' flee empty religion. They then seek after their restored "Relationship" with their Father In Heaven.

Where are the "Relationship" Christians to be found in America today? Those led by the Holy Spirit of God should be busy harvesting lost souls. They should be the <u>united</u> in <u>Love</u> - **Bride of Christ.** Loving others the same way Jesus Loves us. A Bride wearing a garment without the stain of religion, <u>blemish</u> of <u>schism,</u> and without the <u>wrinkle</u> of unloving words and actions toward others. But where is she found in America today?

My job is to call out to the <u>True,</u> having Relationship, walking daily <u>in</u> <u>the</u> <u>Spirit</u> - not in religion, Bride of Christ. I must warn that it is time for you to ARISE IN POWER! BECOME READY AND WORTHY FOR JESUS TO RETURN TO RECEIVE! We in America today are in great danger if we continue allowing our acknowledgement of America's being IN (God) DEPENDENCE, to be slighted as unnecessary. If we continue in powerless apathy over this, could our end as a free and strong nation be far away?

What a price we are already paying. We have allowed those who <u>supposedly</u> "represent" our hopes, needs, and well being, to tax and frivolously spend our money as never before in history. We have elected an immoral man, one bragging about his support for the murder of innocent babies in their mother's womb, to use our "In God We Trust" money to murder children in foreign countries, and more recently, with the "Health Bill," murder babies in our own country. In God We Trust, has already been relocated - to the edge of our coins.

What will it take for God to again get our attention? In the 1860's it was a Civil War. In the Twentieth Century it was World Wars. Will it be terrorist's attacks of inhuman cruelty, the kind pleasing to satan, whom they follow? Will you heed this plea I am now making? Or will you dare God to shake you out of your Apathy and feeling secure in your "old Time Religion"?

I ask these questions **boldly** because now is a time requiring **BOLDNESS!** Apathy won't produce Boldness or results. Religion has not the power to produce Boldness. **SEEK AFTER THE SPIRIT OF TRUTH – THE SPIRIT OF GOD – TO LEAD AND DIRECT YOUR LIFE DAILY. "SEEK FIRST, THE KINGDOM OF GOD AND HIS RIGHTEOUSNESS." VOTE TRAITORS OUT OF OFFICE. SEEK TO BE, TO KNOW, OR TO FIND, MORAL MEN AND WOMEN WORTHY OF RUNNING FOR POSITIONS OF AUTHORITY IN AMERICA. THEN BE SURE TO SEEK DISCERNMENT, BEFORE YOU CAST YOUR VOTE.**

Cowards will try to tell you its too late. In addition to being Cowards, they are LIERS! As long as we are willing to work, work hard at restoring the meaning of In (The One True) God We Trust, in the hearts of America's people, there is still hope for God to restore us as a Great nation again. But should we fail, all must pay the horrific cost!

Am I seeking for America to be like Iran, as it was and is under clowns like the late Ayatollah Ko Maniac, and its current man of darkness (I'm A Did A Scam)? This is what the fans of satan will declare about me. Nothing could be further from the truth. Iran is a perfect example of what happens to a country under the false god of Religion.

I seek to see America under the guidance of the ONE TRUE GOD. He is a God of Love - not Hate; of Light - not darkness; a Loving Father - not a demonic Jerk! This is my defense to those lying about what I desire for America to become. I would love to see the America which I grew up in restored. An America, whose people desire the Freedom to Worship, Love, and Serve, the One **True** God. To see this greatness restored once more in the hearts of America's people and its leaders, this is my goal.

If my prayers are granted, America will end the murder of little babies for convenience, and again will become a Great nation, Under the One True God, In Whom We Trust.

Chapter Thirteen
DO YOU HAVE FAITH ENOUGH TO FACE THE LION?

How the Christian church in America has grown in cowardliness, rather than in Faith! Some time ago in our history, tyrants in business declared the Commandment of God to be null and void. What Commandment, you may ask, the Commandment regarding keeping Holy the Lord's Day. For many decades, honoring this Commandment was sacred to American's. They still knew and loved the One True God. To Catholics, going to church on Sunday was a sacred "DUTY."

To others, Sunday presented not a duty, but an "OPPORTUNITY." It was the opportunity to Worship and Praise God collectively. It was opportunity to show God you loved Him, enough to honor His Commandment. It was also an opportunity to grow in spiritual maturity, as you heard the Word of God taught. Sunday's were also an opportunity to have any wounds healed. Wounds you may have suffered during the week, as a fiery dart hit you while lowering your shield of Faith, when in battle. Sunday also brought you the opportunity to get your Faith charged up, to give you the energy and power to go forth into battle again.

Yes, this was the Sunday in which Christians of sixty years ago in America offered reverence, respect, and honor to the One True God. The One in Whom we supposedly put our trust. The One Whom we supposedly pray to in Faith. The very fact that Sundays were revered as the Lord's Day spoke volumes about the Christians of sixty years ago and before.

But then something changed in the hearts of Americas Christians. The tyrants of business, in their greed, declared that no longer is Sunday the Day of the Lord. NO! It now became a day of greed! A day in which the business owners could gain more money! **MONEY**, the god of many businessmen, became the new standard we were to honor, reverence, and respect. And one by one they fell!

At first, not all business owners went along with this apparent greed. There were the hold outs. There were also pastors who spoke out against this evil practice. They urged the sheep under their care not to participate or go along with this evil desire to take Sundays away from honoring God. But, just as with the businessmen, one by one they fell too.

First, an incentive of time and a half, or even double pay, was offered to those willing to work on Sundays. The dollar signs began to light up in the eyes of those calling themselves Christian. In the beginning, the hold backs refused, at least until seeing the huge difference in pay of their co-worker who worked Sundays. Then greed took over. They started planning the nice vacation they could take with this "extra" money or it may have been the new car, refrigerator, washer, etc. this "windfall" could now give.

What about those Pastors, preaching so vehemently against business being open on Sunday? satan offered the perfect way of dealing with them. It is called the "One Day Only Sale'! It goes like this: This SUNDAY ONLY, from Noon till Six P.M. Washer & Dryer Combo, regularly $1,400.00 JUST $1,000.00! Save $400.00 TODAY ONLY – Between Noon and Six P.M.! HURRY! Pastor's wife said: "George, we could use a new washer and dryer. Did you see this ad in the paper today? They're offering $400.00 off, but it's only good Sunday."

Starting at 10:30, the church service which normally lasted until noon suddenly was over by 11:00. Next, that Pastor and his wife were seen standing in line outside the business' door, waiting for noon, to run in and purchase that washer & dryer at a great savings. They had sold out, and were instantly open to the criticism of being labeled a "hypocrite" by others, particularly by the "sheep" in their care. Satan through compromise had them where he wanted them – unable to speak out against stores choosing to open on Sundays.

It's hard to believe it was sixty years ago when Sunday, and respect for God's Commandment through obedience, came under attack by the greedy tyrants of business. Compromise became the operative word. The businesses offered to keep the hours of "only" noon to six P.M. as their standard. Pastors began to "adjust" their services to help their "flock" who had to be at work, make it on time. The Catholic Church among others, began to set up services for a different day, Saturday, proclaiming it to be the "new" "Lord's Day." God, and honoring ONLY Him, got left in the dust somewhere. Greed had won!

It is sad to say, I was one of those Christians who at first abhorred the very idea. Sundays had always been a day of serving God and of rest. I was at first very upset. Then I started looking at the pay difference, and said, "It won't hurt to work just one Sunday a month to gain some "extra" **money**. After all, working on Sunday's is strictly "voluntary." It's not like they are forcing it on us. No, at first no force was used. You could not be threatened with the loss of your job, as it was purely "voluntary" on the part of the worker.

What a big lie and sad joke was played on the working force, and we fell for it! Where is the "Purely Voluntary" policy today? Today, it is either be here, or be FIRED! Today, we have learned the business owner "owns" the worker. The business first, God and church come last! Today, you cannot even wish anyone a Merry Christmas. Because that evokes images of the

One Who came from Heaven to save mankind from our sins. What an awful and offensive image! Today, Sunday, Easter and Christmas, are treated as just another work day. We sit by in apathetic silence, while asking God to Bless America. Does that make any kind of sense?

I think back now, to a much earlier time in the life of the Christian church. By the term Christian church, I'm not referring to "Religious Labels," but to the Christian people – they are "the church." As we know, early Christians faced much persecution for their Faith in Jesus. A large number of the early Christians were given a choice: "Reject your Faith in this Jesus, or..... be fed to the lion!" The answer given by the majority was: "Bring on your lion!"

What of the Christian of today? How soft and easy we have it in America. Yet do we today possess the courage and Faith to say: "Bring on your lion?" That greedy business man or woman is the lion of today. The one declaring, you MUST work for ME on Sunday – I want more wealth! Forget about honoring, serving, or worshipping your God! I am your God, and money is my god!

Our past history is a sad statement of Faith. I, like others calling them selves a "Christian" said, I will reject my Faith in honoring the One True God. I will accept honoring you and your silly god of money. I am guilty of having done this, so please do not think I am throwing stones at anyone.

It's just the fact that a particular Scripture has been haunting me. It is a warning issued by a God, Who loves us. "Do not **forsake** the assembling of yourselves together; particularly as you see the "last days" approaching." Do we see the "last days" approaching? The answer to that is a "no brainer." Of course we do! How greatly I admire Mr. Truitt Cathy, owner and founder of Chick-fil-a. He refuses to open on Sundays, choosing instead to honor God's Commandment. Mr. Cathy is a worshiper of the Lion of Judah!

But the lions of greedy businessmen and women need to be faced with Faith, not Fear, by we who call ourselves "Christian." The lion of today is the one saying: YOU MUST WORK ON SUNDAYS - IF YOU WISH TO STAY EMPLOYEED BY ME! Does that sound a bit like a Threat? The little lion's roaring comes from the mouth of the empty headed god of greed. Is this something we should fear? Where is your gift of FAITH Christian? Will you continue deserting God out of fear? Do you fear persecution for desiring to obey the Commandment of God?

Sadly, from the 60's on, the answers have been: Yes, I take their threat seriously, I fear loosing my job. My faith is hidden. It's something personal, between God and me. God will understand why I have to work and miss church on Sunday. I don't believe I would like being persecuted. I know I won't be, if I don't give them (the heathen) a chance to find a reason.

Perhaps here, it would be good for me to define the word heathen, as I use it. A **heathen** is one who knows of the One True God. They know He is a God of Love, Light, and Abundant Life. Yet they in ignorance choose to reject Him, following instead, one of satan's gods of hatred, darkness, despair, and death; or one of the many gods of man's imagination; or in some cases, no god at all. To me, a heathen, is someone who has unwisely tossed aside God's gift of faith, to accept a false, empty headed (such as there is NO God), and phony lie from satan

Although through the grace of God, I never chose to become a heathen, still I have been one of the cowards of the past, fearing to take a stand against working on Sundays. Today, as CEO of Fire of Love Books LLC, I have no fear my boss would fire me for not working on Sunday. I may be criticized for making the bold challenge I am about to make. I will be called "Safe" and "Secure," having my little Social Security check each month.

I am willing to risk such criticism, because I know my job is using the Words of God, to warn LOUDLY and CLEARLY concerning these "last days." We are NOT to **FORSAKE** the assembling of ourselves together! This warning could apply to everyday of the week. I know this. But I say, let us take back our right to honor the Commandment of God. Let us insist on no work on Sundays! I know there are exceptions, such as police, hospitals, and firemen, to name just a few. But such work is work motivated by compassion and caring about others, and not about greed!

Do you realize until the 60's there existed in a majority of states, a thing called the "blue laws"? They stated no contract entered into on a Sunday would be honored. People ask what kind of nuts would have made such a law. Only Christians who truly sought to honor the One True God, more than money and greed. Those who made such a law are long dead, as is observance of the law they made.

I ask of the Christian of today: Are you also dead? Or is it just your Faith that is dead? Are you willing to suffer persecution if it means the loss of your job? What a **BOLD** question to ask, particularly in a time when the loss of jobs is happening at an alarming rate! We have an inept President who blows smoke and hot air from a teleprompter. We have an effort being made to destroy the value of our money through going into enormous debt. Now you dare to ask me to risk loosing my job? Why, to place God first in my life? Man, I NEED my job, and that money. How would I live?

These are all important questions which need answering. So I will attempt to answer each one. First, have you ever considered the tough economical time we are going through could be partly because we have dishonored God, placing Him last in our society today? Do you really believe God is thrilled by our having turned authority to govern, over to heathens? Putting God first in your life is only relevant, if obeying the eleven commandments is important to you. If not – don't call yourself a "Christian;" because your fruit reveals only a label wearing "powerless," "religious" person. Placing God first in your life is something done by those sharing a loving "Relationship" with God, through Jesus, and by God's Holy Spirit.

Now it's time to address what are your most urgent and true needs. You need not to remain a "Baby" or a "Childish" Christian for all of your life. You need to grow up, into spiritual maturity, and "become" the spiritually mature son or daughter God desires to see you grow to become. Check it out! Read John, Chapter one, verse twelve (in the King James Version – not one of the watered down versions!) How do you grow up to become the spiritually mature son or daughter of God? In Romans, 8: 14, we are told: "For as many as are led by the Spirit of God, they are the sons (and daughters) of God."

But lets get down to the meat of the problem, how to get your needs met by God. "Seek first, the Kingdom of God and His Righteousness; and all you truly have need of, will be provided." What is the Kingdom of God? "The Kingdom of God consists of Righteousness, Peace, and Joy – IN THE HOLY SPIRIT!" Where is the Kingdom of God? Well, if you are truly born again by the Spirit of God, God's Kingdom is within you. The problem is: we must choose dwelling within the Kingdom of God, not that of satan, the world, or our flesh.

Guess what? Shocking news flash! When you choose honoring greed more than God, when you fear the little lion of businessmen and women, more than you have Faith in God, you are choosing to dwell in the kingdom of satan (because you place God last), your flesh (because you want money), and the world (because you plan on what that extra money can bring you in the world). Isn't it time you tried dwelling in the Kingdom of God?

I say, and boldly challenge, it's time to take back Sunday, and give it wholeheartedly to the Lord. If we do, as a reward, our economy could miraculously recover. But we will never know this is true, without our actions of FAITH! We have is God's promise. He is a REWARDER of those who DILIGENTLY SEEK Him. For those possessing "Relationship" Faith, that is enough to have no fear. For all possessing only religious faith, (which allows you to remain a child, being tossed to and fro by every wind of man-made doctrine and dogma of pride and division), it is not enough.

Reader, dare I ask, which are you? Do you have and daily share a loving "Relationship" with your Dad, through the guidance of His Holy Spirit in your life? Or do you only possess "powerless religion," which offers a form of Godliness, but denies the Power thereof (which is the Holy Spirit). "Nevertheless, when the son of man returns; shall He find Faith on the earth?" This is the question posed by Jesus. Religious faith, which offers only man-made doctrines, dogmas, and traditions of pride and division, are not of the Spirit of Truth. Faith which is possessed by those enjoying the loving "Relationship" which Jesus came to earth to "restore" between man and our Dad, Who is in Heaven, leads a Christian to know no fear when opposing satan, and those in service to him.

Are you ready to be persecuted for your faith? Are you willing to risk loosing your job in a tight economy, to prove God comes first? Is the source for your Faith to be found within the Kingdom of God, or within those other empty and powerless kingdoms of satan, the world, or our flesh? Do you have faith enough to face the lying lion? It's time for you to reveal the true answer, especially if you choose calling yourself a Christian. "By their "Fruit" you will know them."

Look at the reality of what I am asking, before you make your decision. I am asking that you risk being fired, for the simple reason that you Love God more than money. I am asking that you seek FIRST dwelling within the Kingdom of God each day – job or no job! I am asking if you are willing to suffer persecution for the sake of the Gospel of Jesus Christ. Businessman and woman, many of these questions apply also to you. Do you really think putting in 10% of your Sunday take, will exempt you from being held accountable for all you have turned away form seeking, serving, and loving the One True God? If you have your faith in this lie of satan, you are skating on very thin ice my friend.

Let them dare to fire you! I say, "Fire back!" Get a good CHRISTIAN Attorney to represent you, and go after any who dare to challenge your "religious freedom." Do you think the ACLU (anti-Christian Lawyers Union) would be interested in helping you win your case? Don't bet on it! They are only interested in the "religious freedom" of any and every flakey god of satan and man's imagination, which opposes the One True God. Who needs the help of such "Spiritually Challenged individuals? Unfortunately, not knowing or willing to receive the True God into their heart, sadly, they are useless.

The Commandments of God supersede those of an oppressive and would be "Godless" government. Our founding fathers knew this was so. This is why they founded America on the principle that our government (unlike the one they had fled from) would have absolutely NO AUTHORITY to impose loss of freedom, in when and how we choose worshipping the One True God (they even threw in all of the false gods, so the ACLU would be happy). The law is on our side. This "so called" division of church and state is found in the manifesto of Karl Marx, **not** in our beloved Constitution!

Our freedom in choosing when and how we serve the One True God, is not, and never should be at the mercy of either government, or greedy businessmen or women! It is time this TRUTH was made evident! But how many have the Faith it will take to make this happen? I tell you in truth, I would have absolutely no fear or remorse in suing any employer who chose to fire me for desiring to place my God (the One TRUE God), above them and every other little god or "would be" tyrant. I would sue, and wind up owning their company. Then every employee would have EVERY Sunday off. How about this? Every employee would be encouraged to wish a Merry Christmas and a Happy Easter to everyone! Try to make me stop – I DARE YOU!

O.K. satan, bring on your little minions with their criticism! Sure, Joe, it's easy for you to talk BIG. You own of a Christian business, are a moderately successful author, and have a monthly Social Security check to look forward to receiving. Where were you earlier? Sadly, earlier I did not possess the kind of Faith I needed, nor understood how important the quality of the Relationship I share with God each day is to me. But now I do. I do not wish to see others travel down the same dumb path I was on for so many years of my life. God either is Lord of your life or not! It's that simple!

In my old days of being trapped in "powerless religion," I felt safe and secure warming a pew for a little while on Sundays and counting on the label of my "Religion" to get me through the gates of Heaven. Then later, even after becoming born again by the Spirit of God. I fell for the same simple minded game many ministers play on their congregation. I put a period where there was only a comma. "There is therefore no condemnation for those who are in Christ Jesus" Period? I don't think so! How about that stuff which follows after the COMMA? "who walk not in the flesh, but in the Spirit (of God)." St. Paul said: "If we say we have the Spirit of God inside, should we not walk in the Spirit?"

Taking away that period which does not belong, and listening to the words which come after the comma, has made a drastic change in what makes me feel safe and secure. I hope in reading this, it will make the same kind of difference in your perception as well.

It is time we take on the tyrants, and face the lions in America today. It is time we fight for, take back, and restore the precious freedoms given us by our founding fathers. It is more than time we returned the One True God to His place of prominence over the false gods of satan and man. It is time for FAITH to be something Jesus will find ALIVE in ABUNDANCE in the hearts of the people living in the one country of the world which was dedicated to Him. One Nation Under God is our true motto. The very idea of One Nation under false gods or tyrants should be buried and abolished once and for all in America.

How may we do this, you may be asking. Simply by loving those who do not know the One True God, into His Kingdom; by demonstrating the power of producing the Fruit of the Spirit in our daily life; by living as the just choose to live ("The just, shall live by FAITH"); and by choosing each day to seek first to dwell within the Kingdom of God (this is how we are in the world, yet not part of it). Do you possess the kind of Faith which will allow you to do these things without fear? Or do you only possess powerless "religion"? Your response and your actions will reveal the truth to you. As for my wife and I, "Our house will serve the Lord" (and no other god)!

Chapter Fourteen
IF YOU WERE TO DIE TONIGHT

We know America's health is in critical condition with God being expelled from areas He has been a part of for over one hundred and seventy five years. With "leaders" and "would be judges" telling false gods or "nothingness" (Atheist), you are free to take God's place. With immoral, money grubbing, political liars, replacing God's laws of morality and justice with their own corrupt and immoral ideas, America is on the operating table, gasping for air.

All of this paints a desperate picture. America's fate depends on how skillful and available a surgeon you and I are. Will we succeed in placing Love and Reverence for the One TRUE God back into the hearts of America's people and leaders? Only time will tell, America could die or live tomorrow.

But how about you reader, suppose you were to die tonight, are you prepared? Will your eternal destiny be Heaven or Hell? To where have you sent your treasure ahead? Or is it all being wasted by your selfish life on this earth? Will you be living in a small golden shack or a great mansion in Heaven? With what materials have you chosen to build your eternal home? Or have you chosen a mansion in Hell, the place of eternal torment?

Such questions are good to ask of yourself from time to time. They remind us of the reality that we are spiritual beings, traveling on a journey toward eternity. Where our journey comes to an end is of vital importance. The trials and tribulations we endure in this life are merely opportunities for us to learn how very much God loves us. They also bring us opportunities to store up treasure in Heaven, as we learn to live by Faith and not by sight.

Most of America's founding fathers were able to rest in peace when they died, because they had fought to establish a country where the One True God is free to be worshiped, praised, and adored. What of you and me? If we were to die tonight, would we know we have fought to restore and preserve the precious freedoms of reverence to God given by our forefathers? If so, we too will have peace, just as I am certain Ronald Reagan is at peace today.

Our flesh, which is made of the dust of this earth, is weak and feeble. When we die our body will return to the dust of this earth. But our soul desires to possess an eternal home of Love, Peace, and Joy. Will you have allowed Jesus by His Holy Spirit, to bring your soul safely to that Heavenly home? Or will you have allowed satan to lead you into eternal damnation in Hell?

All of the questions in this chapter are insightful in their nature. They were meant to be that way. Their goal is to ask each reader to take a moment to evaluate where they are in their spiritual walk toward eternity, and where they are headed. If you are troubled by any of the honest answers you gave, it is a good thing. Just as you should be troubled by any dishonest answers you may have given.

Your answers may have revealed to you the need for a change of motive and direction in certain areas of your life. If so, what are you going to do about it? Sure, you could try sweeping it under the rug, attempting to hide it till next year comes around. But suppose for you next year never comes around? The cold hard facts are easy to understand, you **could** die tonight. There is no guarantee on the length of your days on earth. Eternity lies beyond this world. Rich or poor, famous, infamous, or unknown, we all have a date with eternity. Are **you** ready? If not, are you willing to work to get ready?

If you are not ready right now to face eternity, you need to be made aware of a basic truth, satan desires for you to stay in that hopeless, helpless, godless state of apathy. satan fears your coming to the knowledge of the truth concerning Jesus Christ. He knows the Truth will set you free from all of his lies and deceptions. As long as you choose to deny and resist, your body, soul, and spirit receiving the new birth of being born by the Spirit of God, you will stay spiritually dead. I plead with you please do not continue allowing satan to drag you to Hell - his eternal home - to be with him throughout eternity!

satan is really so easy to defeat! Jesus won our victory over satan long ago by the Power of His Precious Blood on Calvary. Will you let the Blood of Jesus free you from all bondage of darkness, apathy, despair, and eternal spiritual death? He desires to do this for you simply because He Loves you! All Jesus asks of you in return is to put your faith and trust in all His sacrifice of Love on the cross did for you and me.

By the Blood of Jesus, your sins are forgiven, completely washed away and forgotten by God. Through the Blood of Jesus, your relationship with your Heavenly Father is restored. In being covered by the Blood of Jesus, you can receive and know the Power of being guided by the Holy Spirit of God. What more do you and I need to be able to travel toward eternity with Love, Joy, and Peace reigning in our body, soul, and spirit?

Would you like to experience the reality of the One True God America was built upon? Do you desire to be filled with His Spirit and His Love? If so, please say this simple prayer from the depth of your heart. "Dear Jesus, I am a sinner. With great sorrow I acknowledge the many times I have failed and hurt You. I acknowledge also that this very moment I ask You to come into my life. I honor and acknowledge You to be my Lord, my God, and the Savior of my body, soul, and spirit. Right now Jesus I place my body, soul, and spirit, and their eternal destination into Your hands. I trust in Your Love, and the Mighty Power of Your Blood to forgive me of my every sin, making my life complete and my journey safe. I ask You to baptize me with the Baptism of Your Holy Spirit, and fill me with the Fire of Your Love. Please use me to be an effective witness to others of Your great Love and Power. May I bring many souls with me on my journey toward my eternal home in Heaven. All of this I humbly ask with thanksgiving, in Jesus' name. Amen."

EPILOG

"America is no longer a "Christian" nation." These are the proud and boastful words of what we unfortunately must call "President" for almost four years. We DESPERATELY need to have a NO CONFIDENCE vote available to the voters, for Congress, the Presidency, and Vice Presidency, all the way down to local levels. This way, when the voters mistakenly elect obviously immoral, highly incompetent, "leaders;" proving themselves too ignorant, unwilling, or simply unwise in making decisions effecting the good of the majority; then the majority of voters can fire him or her. Also, any fired this way will immediately become ineligible for any benefits. NO benefits whatsoever, they will have forfeited the right to every benefit, through being a proven failure to those who elected them.

It is up to True, COMMITTED Christians to stir up the gift of the Holy Spirit within. Arise under His guidance and wisdom, and do the work needed to save America from extinction among the free countries of the world. God has promised to pour out His Holy Spirit in these last days. I urge you to become part of that great outpouring. Love others the same way Jesus loves you.

Our work is to introduce our fellow Americans to the One True God. Not the god of darkness which Jeremiah Wright serves & expounds (the one permitting and urging him to use God's name in vane and curse America). Our work is to be a Light in places of darkness, to pull down strongholds of princes and principalities of darkness in the life of our country, and that of our brothers and sisters who are living in bondage to the false gods of satan and man's religions.

I realize this book is short, having just fourteen chapters. But they are fourteen powerful chapters. The well being of America the country we Love, depends on the well being of your body, soul, and spirit, and mine. There really is nothing more to be said, other than, let's go to work! I do wish to offer my thanksgiving to God for having chosen to use this "foolish thing" for His honor and glory. I pray by the Fire of His Love, He will use each reader of this book to make a positive difference in America's future. Let us make America shine again among nations, with the Bright Light of the One True God. May America once again be a Beacon of Hope and Love to the world; and may the One True God live and reign within the hearts of her people, and guide her leaders toward achieving greatness among the nations of the world – Hey Wright! GET IT RIGHT!

It's:

GOD <u>BLESS</u> AMERICA!

www.ingramcontent.com/pod-product-compliance
Lightning Source LLC
Chambersburg PA
CBHW060633280326
41933CB00012B/2029